New
ΓΑVΟ RΙΤΕ$

Classic International Cuisine

Redesigned Recipes for Your Health

by
Brook Katz

New Favorites
Classic International Cuisine
Redesigned Recipes for Your Health

Brook Katz

Published by
Brook's Books, Etc., Ltd.
P.O. Box 880446
Pukalani, HI 96788

brookkatz@hotmail.com

ISBN 0-9676564-2-7

Dedication

*This book is dedicated
to all those who give
their lives;
their time,
their energy,
for the support of
human rights,
animal rights,
and the sustainable rights
of our living planet.*

Bless you all!

In memory of
H. Jay Dinshah
For he was such a man.

Introduction

I decided to write this book to answer the many questions put to me through the years. Whether it's, "where do I get my protein (or calcium, iron, B-12, etc.)?", or, "how can I give up my favorite foods?" I saw people viewing the change to a healthier, more sustainable life-style, as something that was difficult, time consuming, and inconvenient, rather than something of a highly beneficial nature, and I wanted to do something to show that it doesn't have to be that way.

With the recipes in this book, you'll immediately find yourself cutting down on fats, processed sugars and grains, dairy and meat products, chemicals and preservatives. You'll automatically feel better, while discovering a whole new array of satisfying, mouth-watering dishes that will please the most discriminating palates, and take away the misconceptions that healthy food has to be boring and tasteless.

There is much evidence today that a diet based on plant foods, is much more compatible with the human digestive system, as well as much more sustainable for the ecosystem. *"We, today, are creating the tomorrows of the future, based mainly on the food and life-style choices that we select with our present day consciousness."*

My aim is to help change that consciousness. First, by making people aware of the products we use and purchase, buying only those things which don't hurt us or our planet. Second, by creating the foods that people need, or are used to, in ways that are convenient, delicious, and pleasing to all. That is the main focus of this cookbook.

Hopefully you will find many recipes that are familiar to you in this book. You will notice that they are redesigned to look and taste exactly as you remember them, only without all the harmful things that can rob us of our health, and our environment.

So enjoy that pizza with "Moatsarella Cheeze", or "Banana Creme Pie" without feeling guilty that you're cheating yourself, or the world in which you live. Life is to enjoy! So have a delicious, healthy, guilt-free conscience by eating your way towards true enrichment with *"New Favorites."*

Brook Katz

Acknowledgments

The following groups, and companies have been instrumental in helping to create this book, and in helping me in my many efforts and projects. I would like to offer my deepest appreciation to all those involved, and thank them not only for myself, but for all those whom we work so hard to protect, who cannot speak for themselves.

Red Star Yeast Products
433 E. Michigan Street, Milwaukee, 53202

San-J International Inc.
2880 Sprouse Dr., Richmond, VA 23231

Lundberg Family Farms
5370 Church St., P.O. Box 369, Richvale, CA 95974-0369

Imagine Foods Inc.
350 Cambridge Ave., suite 350, Palo Alto, CA 94306

Mark Kastin – Author: "Timeless Thoughts"
(Global Wisdom Publication)

Institute of Nutrition Education and Research
1601 N. Sepulveda Blvd., Suite 342
Manhattan Beach, CA 90266
(310) 374-3733

French Meadow Bakery and Café
2610 Lyndale Ave. So., Minneapolis, MN 55408
(612) 870-4740 or (612) 870-0907 fax

Eden Foods Inc.
701 Tecumseh Rd., Clinton MI 49236

Contents

Foreword

If you are in the process of evolving your dietary choices by reducing meat and dairy products while consuming more wholesome, plant-based foods, you are not alone. Millions of people around the world are realizing that basing their daily food choices upon animal-derived products is a recipe for disaster. Locally, people are moving towards more non animal-based diets for generally three reasons: health, environment, and ethics.

Health

Many medical studies have indicated that meat and dairy-based diets are major culprits in the epidemic of degenerative diseases that plague most industrialized societies. It's hard to name a common, degenerative disease that is not made worse by fatty, cholesterol-laden animal products. Clogged arteries and high blood pressure that lead to heart attacks and strokes, obesity, diabetes, even many forms of crippling arthritis and deadly cancers, are all fueled by the high-fat, low-fiber "food" products that compose the central staples of Western-style diets. Compounding the inherent health hazards in fiberless, fatty foods are the many contaminants commonly found in today's meat and dairy products: pesticides, herbicides, antibiotics, hormones, and deadly bacteria, like Salmonella and E. coli 0:157. Numerous medical studies now document dramatic improvements – even arrest and reversal of diseases previously thought "irreversible" – upon making wholesome, plant-based foods the central focus of the diet. The start of better health can be as close as your next meal.

Environment

Industrial-scale production of animal products has resulted in mass deforestation, soil erosion, appalling contamination of surface rivers, streams, and underground aquifers, as well as massive air pollution from burning millions of barrels of oil in order to run tractors, trucks, irrigation pumps, slaughterhouse refrigeration units, and freezers. Plant-based diets require far less land, water, and energy to produce, which, in turn, can permit the forests to grow back and the topsoils to stabilize. Thus, as people adopt vegetarian dietary styles, they promote the healing of the global ecology upon which we all depend.

Ethics

As sensitivity to the preciousness of all life increases around the world, the inescapable cruelty inherent in meat-based diets is motivating many people to change their food choices. It is becoming ever harder to deny that purchasing a plastic-wrapped piece of animal muscle in the supermarket inevitably condemns sentient creatures like cows, hogs, chickens, turkeys, and other nonhuman animals to shortened lives in conditions of dismal suffering which end only in the bloody terror of the slaughter-house. More and more people who purchase and consume animal products are realizing that the most effective step they can take to stop the suffering is to refrain from fueling the hideous process with their purchases of meats and dairyproducts. It seems no coincidence that clearer arteries, cleaner air and water, and even a clearer conscience, are all benefits from liberating our diets and our dinner plates from animal products.

Enter Brook Katz

Yet, for most people, the thought of a "balanced" meal without a piece of meat as the central feature is unthinkable. What can we use to fill up "the hole" in the middle of the plate that used to be occupied by steaks, chops, chicken breasts, and fish fillets? What do we pour on our morning cereal instead of cow's milk, and what could ever take the place of beef in the burger? If these questions have prevented you from moving into vegetarian-style eating, you'll be glad to learn you have a friend in Brook Katz.

This enthusiastic and thoroughly lovable man has dedicated himself to creating a truly gentler, healthier, and more compassionate world; and one with great tasting food! Calling upon years of experience in helping people transition to plant-based diets without feeling deprived, he delights in revealing the "secrets" of vegetarian cuisine. Hearty seitan stews, chewy burgers, tofu dishes, no cheese "cheesecake", satisfying soups and salads – all delicious and free of cholesterol, are his specialties.

In the pages that follow, Brook will help you explore the rich and varied cuisine that is available to those who base their diets around plant-based foods. Far from being a diet of deprivation, the recipes in *"New Favorites"* will surprise and delight you with meals that are delicious, convenient, and easy to prepare. If everyone ate in the manner set forth in *"New Favorites"*, they would have far less need for the professional services of physicians like me – which is what I and all healers in their hearts truly wish. So I congratulate you on your interest in better eating and I encourage you to enjoy your journey into this wonderful plant-based cuisine. With Brook Katz as your guide, you won't be disappointed...

Michael Klaper, M.D.
Physician, and Author of:
***"VEGAN NUTRITION: PURE AND SIMPLE "* and**
"PREGNANCY, CHILDREN, AND THE VEGAN DIET"

Abbreviations, Weights, Measurements & Metric Conversions

Abbreviations

g. = gram
lb. = 1 pound
ml. = milliliter
L. = liter
tsp. = teaspoon

Tbsp. = tablespoon
oz. = 1 ounce
pt. = 1 pint
qt. = 1 quart
gal. = 1 gallon

Measurements

Volume

3 tsp. = 1 Tbsp.
2 Tbsp. = 1 oz.
4 Tbsp. = 1/4 cup
8 Tbsp. =1/2 cup
16 oz. = 1 lb.

Fluid

1/2 cup = 4 fluid oz.
1 cup = 8 fluid oz.
2 cups = 1 fluid pt.
2 pints = 1 fluid qt.
4 quarts = 1 fluid gal.

Metric Conversions (approximate)

1/4 tsp. = 1 ml
3/4 cup = 180 ml
1/2 tsp. = 2 ml
1 cup = 250 ml
1 tsp. = 5 ml
1 pt. = 500 ml
1 Tbsp. = 15 ml

1/4 cup = 60 ml
1/3 cup = 75 ml
1/2 cup = 125 ml
1 qt. = 1 L
4 oz. = 115 g.
8 oz. = 225 g.
1 lb. = 450 g.

Oven Temperature Conversions

Fahrenheit	Celsius	
200+	85 -110	low heat
250+	110 -135	
300+	135 -160	
350+	160 - 185	medium heat
400+	185 - 200	
450+	210 - 220	
490+	230 - 250	high heat

Nutrient Food Guide

I am constantly asked questions like, "Where do you get your protein?" or "Where do you get your iron?" So to make things simple for you, here are a few suggestions in each category to give you an idea of how easy it is to make sure you get the proper nutrients your body needs.

Protein-Rich Foods

soybeans
chickpeas
nuts
peanuts
tofu
tempeh

cashews
lentils
sunflower seeds
whole grains
dark leafy greens
beans & sprouts

Iron-Rich Foods

apricots (dried)
chickpeas
dark leafy greens
artichokes
most seeds
nutritional yeast (Red Star)

molasses
sea vegetables
beets
spinach
whole grains
legumes

Calcium-Rich Foods

dark leafy greens
almonds
tofu (precipitated with calcium)
sesame seeds

chickpeas
tahini
legumes
soy & nut milks

Vitamin B-12
sea vegetables
Red Star nutritional yeast (Model T-6635+)
unwashed mushrooms
unpasteurized fermented products
fortified cereals
B-12-fortified soy/rice milks

Omega 3 Oils

flax seed oil
canola oil
walnuts

hemp seed oil
evening primrose oil
pumpkin seeds

Note: Try to include at least one large helping of one or more of the above B-12 containing products at least three times per week. It is thought that some vitamin B-12 is destroyed through washing vegetables with chlorinated water. Spraying with agricultural chemicals also probably reduces vitamin B-12 found on fresh produce.

Consequently, it is wise to eat as much organically-grown food as possible, preferably washed in non-chlorinated water. A diet based upon whole grains, legumes, nuts, seeds, fruits, and dark green leafy vegetables, as well as a reliable source of vitamin B-12 such as those listed above, combined with ample fresh water, exercise, sunshine, and laughter – will provide all the essential vitamins, minerals, and other nutrients that the human body requires.

Setting Up Your Pantry

The following items you will find useful to always have on hand in your cupboards. These include staple items, found in natural food stores, that might have to be refrigerated upon purchase or once they have been opened:

Agar agar: A dried sea vegetable product used for thickening and making gelatins.

Cous cous: A fast cooking grain that's easy and tasteful. Store dry and keep well sealed.

Ginger root: Warming, tangy-tasting root. Can be stored in dark, cool, dry place for moderate amounts of time.

Millet: Highly nutritious grain with a corn/nut kind of taste.

Mirin: Japanese sweetened cooking rice wine.

Miso: Fermented soybean paste. Adds a rich, salty flavor to soups, stocks, dressings, and sauces.

Mustard: Many prepared varieties are available; choose your own favorite.

Nutritional yeast: A nutritional flavoring. A primary yeast with a cheesy, nutty flavor. High in nutrients especially vitamin B complex. Red Star brand (T-6335+) also supplies B-12.

Oils: I recommend cooking with olive, canola, or sesame oils, and using flaxseed, hempseed, and most other oils in their natural state. (Buy and store all oils in opaque or dark containers and keep cool or refrigerate. This reduces oxidation and rancidity and keeps the oils fresh.)

Quinoa: (pronounced keen-wah) A delicious high protein grain that's low in fat and high in nutrients.

Rice: There are many tastes and varieties available of this grain. The organic whole grains are more nutritious. Choose any of Lundberg Families' delicious wide range of rices.

Sweeteners: Maple, rice, corn, and malt syrups, and raw date, cane or coconut sugars. There's also sorghum, molasses, fructose, stevia and fruit concentrates.

Sea Vegetables: Kombu, dulse, kelp, arame, wakame, nori, etc. High in vitamins and minerals, especially iodine. Gives a fishlike taste to dishes. Powdered kelp is a good salt replacement.

Spices and Herbs: A long list of varieties – they are used for flavoring, coloring, and enhancing the aromas of whatever you're cooking. They can be used fresh, or dried and stored. Keep your favorites on hand. There are many herbs used for healing as well.

Tahini: Sesame seeds ground into a butter.

Tamari: A rich, salty-tasting fermented soy product. (Try San-J's tamari and also their soy sauce, shoyu, and other sauces).

T.V.P.: (Texturized vegetable protein) A dried chewy soy protein used for a ground meat replacement.

Tofu: The curd of the processed soybean is a good protein and calcium source (when precipitated with calcium chloride – see the package label). An extremely versatile ingredient, it can be used as a meat or dairy alternative. Refrigerate fresh tofu. Once the package is opened, place remainder in a container of fresh water and change the water daily. Tofu also comes in foil boxes that can be stored on your pantry shelves for up to 6 months.

Vinegar: Applecider, wine, rice, balsamic, and other flavors. It's a fermented product that gives a tart or sour taste to your favorite sauces, dressings, or soups.

Tofu

An ancient oriental food dating back many centuries, only recently has it come into its own in the Western world. Known also as bean curd, it is commonly used as a staple item in much of the world's diet. It comes from the soybean plant and is rich in protein and calcium, yet low in saturated fat and sodium, and contains no cholesterol. It is also high in phytoestrogens, and has been shown to help fight certain cancers as well. This makes it a perfect alternative to the high fat diet that the average Western meat and dairy based culture is centered around. *Tofu* has a very bland taste in and of itself, but that fact only adds to its advantages and makes it one of the most versatile foods known. It allows it to lend itself to any spices or flavorings that we wish to use with it, and gives us a wide range of choices that we can make with it. *Tofu* can be made into dressings, sauces, desserts, soups, casseroles, patés, dips, spreads – and the list goes on and on, limited only by your imagination.

Tofu is available almost everywhere now. Once found only in health food stores or oriental food shops, it is rapidly becoming mainstream, and now is in almost every major supermarket and grocery store. It is usually in the refrigerated cases, dated and water-packed for freshness. After it is opened, any unused portion should be kept in water and the water changed on a daily basis. There are several companies that now have it vacuum sealed in special containers which allows it to be kept for extended periods, on your pantry shelf as well. This makes it very convenient when you can't get out, or when travelling.

Tofu comes in several different textures depending on your needs. Soft tofu (which breaks apart if you try to pick it up) is good for dressings, soups and sauces. Medium tofu, a bit firmer, is great for cream dishes, pie fillings, yogurt and puddings.

Lastly, firm and extra firm tofu (which you can pick up with no problem) is ideal for cutlets, burgers, omelets, and cheesy fillings. These of course are but a few of the many dishes that can be made from this wondrous product. In this book, you will find many more ideas, but I urge you to experiment and find new and innovative ways of your own to utilize this wonderful food.

Egg Substitutes

Eggs are one of the most concentrated forms of fat and cholesterol that are consumed in the standard Western-based diet. The yolk of that egg is meant to fuel a growing chick for 21 days without any other means. It was never designed to go into the human body as a fuel source. In baking and in cooking, eggs are usually used to hold things together as a binder, like in burger batters and in cake recipes. In cooking, they are usually whipped up and then scrambled into a recipe, again to hold it together.

I find that for these purposes, replacing them with alternatives is no problem. As of yet, I have not found a practical way of duplicating the membrane which holds the yolk in place so that I can replicate "Sunny side up" eggs, but I'm working at it. It's only a matter of time before I or someone else comes up with it. The following list will give you some ideas and guides on what to use in your favorite recipes.

Agar agar: A sea vegetable product that gels to make custards and flans. Boil 3/4 cup of water, add 1 Tbsp. agar agar and stir until dissolved. Remove from heat. Add flavors, seasonings, etc., and allow to cool and set. To use in a recipe, while still in liquid form, add 1 1/2 Tbsp. of dissolved agar agar for every egg called for in the recipe.

Arrowroot: Use as a binder for your creme pies and soufflés. Add 2 Tbsp. arrowroot per cup of water, and flavor it for custards and puddings as a thickener. I don't recommend it for replacing eggs on a one to one ratio.

Cornstarch flour: Mix 1 Tbsp. cornstarch flour with 2 Tbsp. water; that equals one egg white to use in recipes calling for eggs.

"Egg Replacer": Prepackaged boxed products of prepared mixes are available at your local stores.

Flax seed: Combine 1 Tbsp. seed to 2 Tbsp. water in a blender and puree until creamy. Replaces 1 egg white.

Potato starch: Same as cornstarch.

Soy flour: Use in burgers, patties, and baked goods. 1 heaped Tbsp. per egg.

Tahini: Great emulsifier and binder. Use 1 Tbsp. per egg in most recipes. Most tahini does have a distinctive sesame flavor.

Tapioca starch: Use in the same manner as "cornstarch" above. (Use the pearl form for puddings and custards.)

Tofu: Use to replace eggs in quiches, omelets, scrambles, egg salad, and eggs in cake recipes.

Note: Oils can be used as replacement for eggs in some recipes, but why? There are so many other low-fat choices like those listed above.

Milk Substitutes

There are actually a number of good reasons to create substitutes for that white, lactose-laden solution that comes from the udder of a cow. I guess the best one is just plain old common sense. Think about it. We are the only animals on earth that not only drink the milk from other animal species, but continue to feed it to each other even after the nursing period of our lives is over. Also realize that 4-legged, 4-stomached animals require a bovine nursing solution, containing the enzymes, hormones, electrolytes, immune, and other factors designed specifically to turn a baby cow from a 65 pound calf into a 400 pound cow within a year. Does this seem like a rational choice, or one that we've just accepted? Furthermore, there are direct links to many diseases due to the high amounts of fat, sodium, and cholesterol found in cow's milk and the products made from it.

The old myth that cow's milk is a good way to get your calcium is no longer acceptable. Many people also find themselves lactose intolerant, suffering bloating, cramps, and excessive gas each time they consume milk products. This is not a disease! Your body is telling you something very clearly. Dairy products can be a catalyst for inflammations and arthritis in the body, and make breathing problems and allergies worse. Many people also experience higher levels of troublesome mucus during periods of colds, flus, and other infections when dairy products figure prominently in their diet.

Because of it's high fat levels, dairy products may interfere with the action of insulin in diabetics, as well as possibly in anyone else. It has also been shown to contain high levels of antibiotics, stimulants, and growth hormones. These are but a few of the health and scientific reasons for choosing alternatives to cow's milk.

How about some of the others, like, "It makes you fat!" When you gain weight, you don't like the way you feel or look. There is a lot of hidden fat in the dairy products we eat. Things like ice cream, sour cream, cheeses, cream sauces, cream soups, butter (in baked goods especially), and milk, have long been considered good food and treats, but with all the recent information we can clearly see that it's just not a wise food source. So what do we choose? If you still like milk with your cereal in the morning, or a little dab in your morning tea or coffee (both decaffeinated I hope), what's a person to do? Here are several alternative choices you may care to try or investigate further. I consider them all to be a plus compared to their relevant conventional counterparts. They are:

Soy milk: Made from soy beans, today's soy milk products come either powdered or in already-made liquid form. Buy it in a carton at any grocery store just as you would cow's milk. Until you open it, no refrigeration is needed. Use "*Soy Dream*" or "*Edensoy*" in any recipes to replace cow's milk at an even ratio.

Rice milk: Made from rice of course! Usually thinner than a soy milk, but just as good tasting. Personally, for just drinking, or in my cereals, I like this better than soy (but that's just my own taste; you decide for yourself). Find one that's fortified with B-12 like "*Rice Dream*" (same with soy milks) and you'll stay nutritiously happy. Rice milk is usually found in the same section as the soy milk in most of the health food shops, and in some grocery stores.

Coconut milk: Made from the young meat and the liquid of the coconut, blended together. A very rich milk containing a higher level of fat than soy, rice, and other plant milks. Used occasionally, there are no serious health concerns regarding cholesterol, etc. Coconut milk is mostly used for curries, soups, and sauces to make a richer taste.

Seed and nut milks: Any seeds or nuts can be made into a milk. You'll find several recipes in this book. Basically they are made by grinding the nuts/seeds down to a meal, combining them with water and the flavoring of your choice. They are great for cereal in the morning, or to use in baking in place of cow's milk (1 to 1). They will tend to separate more unless you add an emulsifier like lecithin, or a little tahini (sesame seed butter). Not to worry though; if, after sitting in the refrigerator, the nut or seed milk begins to separate, just shake it up and it's ready to be used again. Most nut and seed milks keep 2-3 days in the refrigerator. For less grit in the milks, soak your seeds ahead of time and strain the finished product.

Butter substitutes: I can't say that I'm one to recommend margarine in place of butter. To me, they're both unhealthy saturated fat either way! I advise finding products like "*Spectrum Spread*", made from non-hydrogenated vegetable oil, or use plain unsaturated vegetable oil on your toast, corn, etc. I recommend flax seed oil, hemp seed oil, or evening primrose oil, due to their high content of omega 3 essential fatty acids. Other butter alternatives are avocado, tahini, and other nut and seed butters, as well as bean spreads like hummus. Better still, check out the recipe for soy bean spread (page 91) in this book. You won't believe it's not butter!

Kitchen Equipment

I admit that over the years I've had the experience of cooking in all kinds of kitchens. From some of the finest facilities with every catering instrument and tool imaginable, to the middle of the jungle, rolling mashed roots and potatoes in large Ti leaves, cooking them in the hot coals, and having people go find big banana leaves for plates and two thin branches for chopsticks. Amazingly enough, I feel comfortable doing both. In most people's kitchens the needs fall somewhere between these two extremes. The following is a list of basic things that I think most people will find useful and time saving to have:

Food Processor: This is the number one greatest invention of all time! This machine saves me about 7 or more hours every week, and that really adds up! Food processors are great for making fillings, grinding spices, chopping nuts, grating vegetables, dicing onions, pureeing tomatoes, stirring batters...

Cookware: A good set of pots, pans, skillets, etc., is one of the most essential things you'll own. A good set can be a bit expensive, but it should also be a onetime purchase. The better companies usually offer a lifetime guarantee, and do their own servicing. Stainless steel is always my preferred choice, but a nice cast iron skillet can be a real treat to use if seasoned well and kept oiled. Never cook with aluminum because it tends to leach into the food, and has been linked to several diseases.

Blenders (or Bar Mixers): These are also great little machines to have. They are great for making salad dressings, shakes, gravies, smoothies, nut and seed milks, creamy soups, and a host of many other things. I use blenders to liquefy the ingredients to make my cheesy recipes smooth and creamy. There are many brands of blenders, with many speed options, but most of them still only have three real speeds: slow, medium, and high (regardless of how many buttons they have).

Cutlery (Knives): Any chef will tell you the same thing, that you can leave the rest of the kitchen behind, but take your knives! I travel with mine everywhere I go. You get very attached to the feel of your own knife, and kept sharp, will serve you well for a long time. Again, a good knife, or set of knives, is anything but cheap! Remember though how much you will use them, and how a good sharp knife will save you a lot of time in the kitchen (not to mention it's much safer to use a sharp knife than a dull one). The better knives seem to hold their edge much longer. I find the European companies to be superior in this category, particularly the German and the Swiss (although the Japanese steel in their better knives is also good).

Juicers: These are machines that extract the juice from fruits and vegetables, while leaving the fiber behind. There are many different kinds on the market. Some are only meant for citrus fruits, while others, like the *Champion* juicer, can grate and homogenize as well. These can also be used for making apple sauce, nut butters, and frozen fruit custards, just to name a few.

Mixing Bowls: A good set, varying in size, will always come in handy. I recommend stainless steel over glass or plastic. They won't break, or stain, and they're easy to clean.

Baking Dishes and Trays: Again, stainless steel is my choice, however you'll also find that glass brands like *Corning* or *Pyrex* work really well for small casseroles and bakes, and can take high temperatures in the oven.

Vegetable Steamers: The small basket that fits into a large pot over a small amount of boiling water lets vegetables, grains, and legumes cook above the steamy heat source. A wonderful way to cook your veggies, without boiling away all the nutrients in them. Either stainless steel or bamboo fill the job well. Make sure not to overcook your foods. Steam cooks fast and hot! A good way for reheating, too.

Wooden Tools: These include such items as spoons, rolling pins, and the all important cutting board. Scientists have found that because the wood is so porous it dries much faster than plastics, and therefore actually reduces the growing medium for harmful molds, mildews, and bacteria – providing the board is cleaned well regularly. You may also want a second board so that you can have one for fruit and one for veggies. This will prevent that onion/pineapple or garlic/strawberry dessert taste.

Remember also that every pot and pan loves a wooden spoon or spatula so as to not scratch its surface; personally speaking, it saves my lips all the time. Because it's not a good conductor of heat, it allows you to taste hot things without burning your mouth like you'd do on hot metal. Just be sure to wash the spoon before putting it back in the pot!

Measuring Cups and Spoons: When you're trying to follow a recipe rather than making one up, you'd better be able to duplicate the measurements pretty precisely. A good set of both metric and English-measure spoons and cups will cover all needs. Now you can share international recipes with your friends.

Sieve: A great tool for sifting dry flours and spices together, as well as taking the lumps out.

Colander: For draining beans, pastas, vegetables, and etc.

Can and Bottle Openers: Not that I have much use for either of these items, but you never know. It sure makes things a lot easier if you do have them if they're needed!

Vegetable Peeler: Pretty self explanatory if you ask me. Good for potatoes, carrots, cucumbers, eggplants, etc. ***Note:*** If you get good organic produce try to avoid peeling whenever possible, and wash your vegetables in non-chlorinated water whenever you can.

Baking Accessories: These would include things like: cake pans, baking trays, muffin tins, pie plates, loaf pans, and quiche or flan pans with spring loaded loose bottoms, for serving ease. These should be either glass (except the loose bottom tins), or steel. Do not use aluminum!

Utensils: This category includes steel serving spoons and spatulas, tongs, wire whisks, scoopers, salad servers, skewers, ladles, and other helpful items with which to serve or cook.

Aprons, Pot Holders, and Oven Mitts: I include dish towels and trivets (things to put hot pans and dishes on) in this group as well. Always try to have a second set, so one can be used while the others are being cleaned.

Pastry Brush: This is for brushing oil on top of your pastry crusts, garlic breads, or filo doughs. It can also be used to brush sauces on top of things like BBQ or roasts.

Bean & Legume Preparation Times

Bean	Soaking time	Cooking time
Adzuki	4 hrs. - overnight	approx. 1 hr.
Black	4 hrs. - overnight	approx. 1 1/2 hrs.
Black-eyed pea	No soaking needed	30 - 60 min.
Chickpea (Garbanzo)	4 hrs. - overnight	1 - 1 1/2 hrs.
Fava	overnight	2 - 3 hrs.
Great Northern	4 hrs. - overnight	1 hr.
Kidney	4 hrs. - overnight	1 - 1 1/2 hrs.
Lentil , common	30 minutes	approx. 30 min.
Lentil, green	30 - 60 minutes	approx. 45 min.
Lentil, red	0 - 30 minutes	approx. 20 min.
Lima beans	4 hrs. - overnight	approx. 1 - 1 1/2 hrs.
Navy	4 hrs. - overnight	approx. 2 hrs.
Pea (whole)	4 hrs. - overnight	approx. 45 min.
Pea, (split)	30 min.	0 - 45 minutes
Pinto	4 hrs. - overnight	1 - 1 1/2 hrs.
Red	4 hrs. - overnight	1 - 1 1/2 hrs.
Soybean	overnight	3 - 3 1/2 hrs.

I am reminded of a story I once heard about a dinner party that was being thrown by Count Leo Tolstoy. It seems that, although vegetarian himself, he would regularly invite non-vegetarians over to dine, so they could see the beauty and variety of his diet.

On one such occasion, a particular guest, a countess I believe, was put off by the thought of eating vegetarian and demanded to be served meat with her meal. She was quite insistent about it, so Tolstoy suggested that they take a short stroll while the chef made preparations.

Upon their return they noticed a live chicken tied to the countess' chair with a note on it. The note said that the chef could not bring himself to actually kill the bird, but if the countess would oblige, he would then prepare it and cook it for her.

It is told, happily, that everybody that evening ate a wonderful totally vegetarian dinner.

Breakfast Recipes

Tofu Hawaiian Toast

I came up with this one morning when I didn't quite feel like French toast, but wanted something on that line. Being in Hawaii at the time, it all made sense to me. Hope you like it!

Ingredients:

1 lb. soft tofu
1 1/2 cups coconut milk (canned or fresh*)
2 Tbsp. maple syrup
1 tsp. vanilla
Pinch of sea salt
8 or more slices of a whole grain bread
1/4 cup shredded coconut
Pineapple jam or preserves
Crushed macadamia nuts for garnish
Oil for cooking

Preparation:

In a blender, combine tofu, coconut milk, maple syrup, vanilla, and salt, and blend until smooth. Pour in a bowl, and soak several pieces of bread in it. Heat a small amount of oil in a skillet, and place the coated pieces in the skillet. Cook until both sides are golden brown, repeat until all the batter has been used. Cover each piece with pineapple jam, sprinkle with coconut, and top with macadamia nuts.

Note: For fresh coconut milk, open coconut and drain the water out and place it in a blender. Scoop the coconut meat out and also put in blender. Puree the mixture until smooth, strain if desired, and use. Can refrigerate for up to 2 days.

Makes 4 - 6 servings

No-Oil Date Scones

The perfect dessert. I first designed this recipe for a diabetic friend who really missed out on all the desserts we'd make. She was thrilled, even though she could only eat a little. Nevertheless, she enjoyed it immensely and I'm sure you will too.

Ingredients:

1 cup whole wheat pastry flour
1 cup unbleached flour
1 Tbsp. baking powder
1/3 cup maple syrup and extra for glaze
1 1/2 tsp. cinnamon powder
1/2 tsp. nutmeg powder
1/2 tsp. sea salt
1/3 cup apple sauce
1/3 cup soft tofu - drained
1 Tbsp. tahini
1/2 cup chopped dates (pitted)

Preparation:

Mix all the dry ingredients together. In a processor or blender, combine the tofu, maple syrup, apple sauce, and tahini. Blend until smooth and fold into the dry mix. Add the dates. Stir and blend well, then turn out the batter onto a floured board or table. Knead lightly for about 1 minute, then form into a ball. Press down and flatten to about 1/2 inch thick. Cut pie style into eight pieces. Place on baking paper or lightly oiled tray. Brush with maple syrup and bake at 400° for 15 minutes or until browned.
Serve warm.

Makes 8 scones

Sister's Scrambled Tofu

My very first healthfully prepared food, I remember my sister showing me this one on the day I decided to make that fateful (and blessed) change in my life. I've been passing it on ever since. Hope you do the same! Thanks for sharing it with me, Sis!

Ingredients:

2 Tbsp. canola oil
1 lb. firm tofu - drained
1 medium onion - chopped
2-3 cloves garlic - minced
1 tsp. turmeric
2 Tbsp. San-J tamari
Cayenne or black pepper to taste

Preparation:

In a mixing bowl, mash and combine the tofu with the tamari, turmeric, and pepper, and set aside. In a skillet, heat the oil and sauté the onions and garlic until soft. Add the tofu mix and scramble the ingredients together for several minutes, until everything is thoroughly heated, and the flavors are well mixed. Serve with whole grain toast and your favorite preserves.

Makes 2 - 4 servings

*"He who gains victory over others is strong,
but he who gains victory over himself
is all powerful."*

Lao Tzu

Apple Date Bran Muffins

These no fat muffins are the perfect way to start your day or to give the hungry crowd before dinner – to keep them out of your kitchen!

Ingredients:

2 cups whole wheat flour
1 cup dates - chopped
1 cup bran (oat or wheat)
1 1/2 cups apple juice
1/2 cup maple syrup
1/4 cup canola oil
1 tsp. each - baking powder, baking soda, and cinnamon
1/2 tsp. nutmeg

Preparation:

Soak the bran in the apple juice and set aside. In a mixing bowl combine the dry ingredients together. In a separate bowl combine the remaining ingredients together and mix with the bran/apple mix. Add the dry part and mix together to a stiff batter. Lightly oil a muffin pan and place equal amounts of batter in each muffin hole. Bake in a preheated oven at 350°, for 25-30 minutes or until a toothpick pulls out clean from the center. Cool and turn out onto a rack.

Note: Paper muffin cups will make both removal from the tin and clean up very easy.

Makes 12 muffins

Tofu Omelet

So easy and delicious, it's my daughter's favorite dish to make. I can let her loose, and she can make it all by herself.

Ingredients:
> 1 lb. firm tofu
> 1 tsp. turmeric
> 2 Tbsp. garlic powder
> 1 Tbsp. tahini
> 1 clove garlic - minced
> 1 Tbsp. canola oil
> 1-2 Tbsp. San-J tamari (to taste)
> 1 tsp. nutritional yeast/Red Star

Variations:
Add onions, peppers, mushrooms, olives, tomatoes, etc.

Preparation:
Mash tofu completely in a mixing bowl. Add the garlic powder and tamari, and mix again. Add the tahini and blend. Finally, add the turmeric and mix until everything is colored yellow and the batter holds together well. In a skillet, heat the oil and sauté the garlic. (At this point, you'd add any other veggies of your choice and sauté until just getting soft.) Then fold in the tofu-eggless batter. Mix with the sauté, (and anything else), form into your desired shape, (i.e., circle, heart, star, etc.) Cook on low heat until firm and browned on the bottom and serve. (On nonstick surfaces, turnout on a plate and serve browned side up. Otherwise, use a spatula and flip it over when serving.) Serve this with a "French Meadow" spelt bagel for a totally wheat-free breakfast!

Makes 4 - 6 servings

Rachel's Tofu French Toast

Ingredients:
> 1/2 lb. tofu (soft)
> 1/4 cup water (more if needed)
> 2 Tbsp. tahini
> 1-2 Tbsp. maple syrup/sweetener
> 1/2 tsp. cinnamon and nutmeg
> Pinch of sea salt
> Oil for the skillet (or non-stick surface)
> 4-6 slices of bread (try French Meadow's
>   "French sourdough")

Preparation:
Combine all the ingredients in a blender except bread, and oil. Blend well and pour into a bowl. In a skillet, heat the oil on medium heat. Dip the bread into the batter, coating both sides, and place in the skillet. Cook until golden brown on both sides.

Serve with maple syrup or your favorite organic jams and preserves.

Makes 4 - 6 pieces

"Come, my friends;
it is not too late to seek a newer world.
We are one equal temper of heroic hearts."

Alfred Lord Tennyson

Tofu Western Omelet

Served with toast and juice, it's enough energy to power you through anything.

Ingredients:

> 1 lb. firm tofu (drained well)
> 1/2 cup of any imitation ham flavored meat alternatives - chopped
> 3 cloves garlic - diced
> 1 Tbsp. canola oil
> 1 small onion - chopped
> 1/2 each - red and green peppers chopped
> 1 Tbsp. tahini
> 1-2 Tbsp. San-J tamari
> 1 Tbsp. nutritional yeast/Red Star
> 1 tsp. turmeric powder
> Black pepper or cayenne to taste

Preparation:

In a mixing bowl, mash the tofu. Add the tahini, tamari, yeast, turmeric, and pepper, and mix together thoroughly. Set aside for the moment. In a skillet, heat the oil over a medium flame. Sauté the garlic and onions for one minute. Add the alternative meat product and the peppers, and cook another minute or until the peppers are soft. Fold in the tofu batter and mix everything together well. Turn flame down to low and cook until the bottom is golden brown, shaping it all into a round form. (If you like, use your imagination and shape it into a heart or star or whatever you like.) Remove from heat and serve.

Note: The bottom will be browned, so you may want to serve it upside down so the browned part faces up. Serve with whole grain toast and decaffeinated tea or coffee substitute.

Makes 3 - 4 servings

Milk Alternatives

For the many people who may have different allergies to cow's milk or soy, now you have even more choices. I like "Rice Dream" from Imagine Foods, or you can make a milk out of any nut or seed. All you really need is a good blender. I especially like sunny milk (hulled sunflower seeds). I find it light, very tasty, a good source of calcium, and I can make a quart for about 35 cents. Kind of takes the Moooo out of milk for me!

Cashew Milk

Cashews give a rich sweet milk, and they cream up very well. By using less liquid and a little canola oil you can make a nice dessert cream with this recipe.

Ingredients:
>1/2 cup cashews
>4 cups cold water
>1 tsp. vanilla
>1-2 Tbsp. maple syrup, fructose,or other sweetener

Preparation:
In a blender, combine cashews with 1/2 cup of water and blend on low speed until creamy smooth. Add sweetener and vanilla and blend again. While running, add the remaining water. Serve immediately, or refrigerate. Lasts 2-3 days, but will separate. Just shake or stir well before using again.

Variations:
Use sunflower seeds, pistachios, pine nuts, macadamia nuts, pecans, almonds, or any other nut or hulled seed. ***Note:*** With almonds and some seeds you may have to strain before use.

Makes approximately 1 quart

Tofu Milk

When you need to whip up a quick milk with all the benefits of soy, but without that retail store price tag, try this recipe.

Ingredients:
> 1/2 lb. soft tofu (softer the better)
> 3 cups cold water
> 2 Tbsp. maple syrup/sweetener
> 1 tsp. vanilla
> Pinch of salt

Preparation:
In a blender, combine all the ingredients and blend until smooth. Strain if needed and serve. Refrigerate and use within a couple of days time.

Makes approximately 1 quart

"I will not kill or hurt any living creature needlessly,
nor destroy any beautiful thing,
but will strive to save and comfort all gentle life,
and guard and protect all natural beauty
upon the earth..."

John Ruskin

Soy Milk

Nowadays soy milks are found in almost every food store. They are much lower in saturated fats and have no cholesterol. For those who prefer the savings over the convenience of ready-made soy milks, I'm sure you'll delight in these easy recipes.

Ingredients:

> 1 cup soybeans (soaked, cooked soft, and drained)
> 1 Tbsp. tahini
> 2 Tbsp. sweetener (less if desired)
> 1 tsp. vanilla
> Pinch of sea salt
> 3 cups water (cold)

Preparation:

In a blender combine soybeans and 1 cup water and blend until creamy. Slowly add one more cup of water and blend until smooth. Add the remaining water and other ingredients, and blend another 20-30 seconds. Strain if needed, cool and serve, or refrigerate. Will last 1-2 days in the fridge.

Makes approximately 1 quart

"To see what is right and not to do it,
is want of courage."

Confucius

Coconut Milk

This recipe depends a lot on if you live in an area that is tropical enough to have a good supply of fresh coconuts. You could use canned coconut, but I personally don't recommend it. It's just not the same.

Ingredients:

> 3/4 cup shredded coconut (soaked) or 1 cup fresh coconut meat
>
> 3 cups cold water/or the coco liquid plus the difference in water
>
> 1 Tbsp. coconut sugar or sweetener (you can find coconut sugar in Thai or oriental markets)
>
> Pinch of sea salt

Preparation:

In a blender, add coconut and 1 cup water and blend until smooth and creamy. Add sweetener and salt and blend again. While running, add the remaining water and blend 10 more seconds. Strain if needed and serve.

Makes approximately 1 quart

*"Let he that would move the world,
first move himself."*

Socrates

Tofu Sour Cream

This is an extremely low fat, no cholesterol topping that goes great on your baked potatoes. Drop a large dollop in your favorite bowl of soup or borscht.

Ingredients:
>1/2 lb. firm tofu
>2 Tbsp. lemon juice
>1/4 tsp. sea salt
>Pinch of citric acid
>Enough water to thin

Preparation:
Combine all the ingredients in a blender or food processor and blend until smooth and creamy. Chill and use as needed. Will keep for 2-3 days refrigerated.

Makes approximately 1 cup

*"Goodness is achieved not in a vacuum,
but in the company of other men,
attended by love."*

Saul Bellow

Soups

Black Bean, Spinach & Tofu Soup

"For a spicy Jamaican taste, add a hot pepper or two."

Ingredients:

> 1 cup dry black beans (soaked overnight, rinsed & drained)
> 1 medium onion - chopped
> 2 celery stalks - chopped
> 3 garlic cloves - minced
> 1 tsp. fresh ginger - chopped fine
> 6 oz. spinach - rinsed, dried and chopped
> Juice from 1 lemon
> Freshly ground pepper to taste.
> 1/2 lb. soft tofu
> 1/2 tsp. sea salt
> Fresh chopped parsley for garnish
> 8 cups water

Preparation:

In a large pot, combine water, beans, onion, celery, garlic, and ginger and bring to a boil. Reduce heat and simmer for about 50-60 minutes or until beans are tender. In a skillet, place spinach on low heat and stir frequently, add 1/2 the lemon juice by sprinkling it on, and some fresh pepper to taste. Remove after 2 minutes and set aside. In the blender, pulse the tofu, remaining lemon juice, and salt together. Add water if needed. Set the sour cream aside. When beans are tender, take 1/3 of soup with beans and ladle it into the blender and blend until creamy. Return to the rest of the soup and add spinach. Heat for one minute, ladle into bowls, put a large dollop of tofu sour cream into the center of each bowl, and sprinkle with fresh parsley. Serve immediately with fresh bread and salad.

Makes 6 - 8 servings

Tomato Walnut Soup

If you like tomato soup, you'll love this variation. Meant to be eaten cold as an appetizer, it'll certainly be a big hit with your guests. Serve with a dollop of tofu sour cream for added effect.

Ingredients:

4 large tomatoes - quartered
1 lb. soft tofu - drained
3 Tbsp. lemon juice
1 Tbsp. fresh dill - chopped
2 cloves garlic - minced
Sea salt & fresh black pepper to taste
1 cup walnuts - large pieces
Dill sprigs for garnish

Preparation:

Place tomatoes in a food processor and puree. Add tofu and blend well. Transfer to a bowl and mix in the remaining ingredients (except the garnish). Chill, and serve in bowls sprinkled with the dill garnish. Can also be warmed adding just a small amount of water. Do not overheat.

Makes 4 servings

*"If you judge people,
you have no time to love them."*

Mother Teresa

Creamy Onion Soup

This is an easy one, folks. Good for cold days, or as a meal opener.

Ingredients:
> 2 large onions - sliced thin
> 2 Tbsp. olive oil
> 1/2 tsp. caraway seeds
> 1 lb. soft tofu
> 1/2 tsp. dried savory herb
> 2 cups water/vegetable stock
> 1 Tbsp. nutritional yeast/Red Star
> Sea salt and fresh black pepper to taste

Preparation:
In a skillet, sauté onions, caraway seeds, and savory in oil for about 5 minutes. Add the yeast, sauté, vegetable stock/water, and tofu to a blender and blend until creamy. Heat the mixture in a saucepan until the soup is steaming, but be careful not to let it reach a boil. Season with salt and fresh pepper and serve. Goes great with "French Meadow" rye breads.

Makes 4 servings

"It's a great pleasure to help someone feel better.
It's the greatest pleasure
to watch them help another..."

Brook Katz

Tofu Potato-Leek Soup

I borrowed this one from the French. Note how the yeast in this allows that cheesy flavor, and yet it's very low-fat. With some nut paté and fresh French bread, you can almost see the Eiffel Tower.

Ingredients:

> 1 lb. soft tofu
> 4 cups water
> 4 large leeks - cleaned very well and chopped
> 4 large potatoes - washed and cut small
> 2 carrots - sliced
> 2 Tbsp. nutritional yeast (Red Star)
> 3 Tbsp. San-J tamari
> Cayenne pepper to taste
> Extra water if needed
> 1/4 cup toasted sesame seeds for garnish

Preparation:

Add all the ingredients to a large saucepan, except the tofu and sesame seeds. Bring to a boil, reduce heat, and simmer until the potatoes are soft (about 25-30 minutes). Pour about half the soup and veggies into a blender and puree along with 1/2 the tofu. Then repeat with the 2nd half until all the soup has been pureed and returned to the soup pot. Heat and serve with a sprinkle of sesame seeds.

Makes 8 - 10 servings

Coconut Ginger Soup

Ingredients:

15 oz. can of coconut milk
2 Tbsp. canola oil
1 Tbsp. fresh grated ginger root
2-3 garlic cloves, diced
1 medium onion - peeled and sliced in half moons
2 stalks celery - sliced on the bias (including leaves)
1/2 lb. tofu (hard) - cut in small cubes
2 carrots - sliced on the bias
1/2 tsp. ginger powder
1/2 tsp. onion powder
1/4 tsp. garlic powder
1 quart of water
Sea salt to taste
Optional: 2 cups diced chard, spinach, or other fresh
garden green

Preparation:

Place oil in the bottom of a large soup pot, add the diced
garlic and grated ginger root, and sauté until golden brown.
Add onions, celery, and carrots, and sauté until onions are
translucent. Add the water and bring to a soft boil, adding
the tofu chunks at this point. Boil the tofu for 10 minutes.
In a blender, blend 1 cup of coconut milk and 2 cups water
from the stock pot with the seasonings. The ginger is the
main flavor in this soup, so be generous, but don't overdo it.
Repeat the process with the remaining stock and return
it all to the soup pot. Stir and simmer for half an hour or
until the flavors blend. This is not a very thick soup (add
water if necessary). Add greens 10 minutes before
removing from the heat.

Makes approximately 2 quarts

Salads

Garbanzo &
Balsamic Vinegar Salad

I first tasted a similar dish when I was in Northern Africa years ago. The balsamic vinegar gives it a new twist that I really like.

Ingredients:

> 2 cups dry garbanzo beans (soaked overnight, cooked, and drained)
> 2 carrots - grated
> 1 medium beet - grated
> 2 green onions - chopped
> 1/4 cup fresh parsley - chopped fine
> 1-2 cloves garlic - minced
> 2 Tbsp. tahini
> 2 Tbsp. balsamic vinegar
> 1 Tbsp. water
> Sea salt and fresh black pepper to taste

Preparation:

In a mixing bowl combine beans, carrots, beets, onions, and parsley together. In a separate small bowl, whisk together the remaining ingredients and pour over the bean mix. Toss well and serve over crisp garden greens.

Makes 4 servings

Avocado & Black Bean Salsa

This treat pleases kids and adults alike. I like to have the kids help with this one cause it's so easy for them to make. A lot of fun to eat too! Makes a great snack or appetizer.

Ingredients:
> 1 ripe avocado - cubed
> 2 cups dry black beans - soaked overnight, cooked soft, and drained)
> 1 cup of your favorite salsa or see the recipe for *Quick & Easy Fresh Salsa* (page 55)
> Sea salt and fresh ground black pepper to taste.

Preparation:
Combine the first three ingredients together and toss well. Adjust the salt and pepper to taste. Serve with your favorite corn chips or rice cakes.

Makes 4 - 6 servings

"Our medicine should be our food,
and our food should be our medicine"

Hippocrates

Three Bean Sweet Mustard Salad

This salad is low in fat, but high in protein. A real complement to any grain burger or casserole. The sweet and sour flavor is a hit at any meal. Kids really seem to love it!

Ingredients:

- 2 cups small pinto beans (soaked overnight, cooked soft, and drained)
- 2 cups kidney beans (soaked overnight, cooked soft, and drained)
- 2 cups green beans (cooked soft and sliced into 1 inch pieces)
- 1 red onion - sliced and cut in crescent shapes
- 2 stalks of celery - diced
- 1 Tbsp. olive oil
- 3 Tbsp. balsamic vinegar
- 1 1/2 Tbsp. Dijon mustard
- 1 Tbsp. San-J tamari
- 2 Tbsp. maple syrup
- 1 tsp. nutritional yeast/Red Star
- 2 Tbsp. water
- 1 tsp. dry basil

Preparation:

In a large bowl, combine the beans, onion, and celery together. In a separate bowl, whisk all the remaining ingredients together and pour over the bean mix. Toss well and chill. Allow at least 30 minutes or more for the flavors to marry. Toss again several times before serving to allow the flavors to mingle. Serve at room temperature.

Makes 6 - 8 servings

Asian Lentil & Mango Salad

A real feel of the tropical Asian foods of Thailand and Myanmar (Burma). Make this when mangoes are in season and plentiful. Complements Indian cuisine superbly, too! I like to mix my own spice blends and curries. I like to buy them in bulk and always have plenty on hand.

Ingredients:

2 cups dry lentils - washed and cooked until soft
2 ripe mangoes - peeled, seeded, and chopped
1 medium red onion - chopped
2 stalks of celery - chopped
1 red pepper - seeded and chopped
2 Tbsp. canola oil
1/4 cup lemon or lime juice
2 Tbsp. fresh cilantro - chopped
2 tsp. ground cumin
1 tsp. coriander
1 Tbsp. chili powder (less if you want it milder)
Sea salt and fresh ground black pepper to taste

Preparation:

In a mixing bowl, combine the lentils, mangoes, onions, and red pepper together. In a separate bowl, whisk all the other ingredients together and pour over the lentil mix. Toss well and serve chilled or at room temperature. Serve over rice or a bed of lettuce.

Makes 6 servings

Chickpea & Cucumber Salad

Here's a light little number, good for hot summer days. The salad part will keep you feeling light while the chickpeas give you that full, satisfied feeling.

Ingredients:

> 2 cups chickpeas (soaked, cooked, and drained)
> 1 large sweet onion - chopped
> 4-5 cucumbers (Kirbys or pickling size) - peeled and coarsely chopped
> 2 large tomatoes - chopped
> 2 Tbsp. olive oil
> 2 Tbsp. cider vinegar
> 1/2 cup fresh basil - chopped fine
> Sea salt and fresh ground black pepper to taste
> 2 Tbsp. nutritional yeast/Red Star

Preparation:

In a large mixing bowl, blend the oil, vinegar, salt, and pepper together. Add the remaining ingredients and toss thoroughly. Chill and serve.

Makes 4 servings

"Experience is the raw material of science."

Buckminster Fuller

Tofuna Salad (Mock Tuna)

*When my mother first showed me this recipe I was blown away!
I used to like tuna fish. This is so close it's scary. The secret is to
freeze the tofu. It gets a more chewy consistency and kind of
crumbles. The fish flavor comes from the sea vegetables. Easy,
huh? This is one of those dishes that really tastes better the next
day, so plan this in advance. Thanks, Mom!*

Ingredients:

> 1 lb. firm tofu - frozen and drained
> 1 large stalk celery - diced
> 2 green onions - minced
> 1/2 cup vegan/non-egg mayonnaise
> 2 Tbsp. San-J tamari
> 1 Tbsp. lemon juice
> 2 Tbsp. kelp/dulse sea vegetable powder

Preparation:

Thaw the tofu and squeeze out the moisture. Crumble
it into small pieces. Add the celery and green onions.
In a small bowl, mix together the mayo, tamari, lemon
juice, and kelp powder. Add to the tofu mixture and mix
well. Allow it to sit for at least 30 minutes or more to allow
the flavors to marry.

Makes 6 servings

Tofu Cucumber Boats

These are the perfect accompaniment for that special luncheon, or if you want to get kids to like cucumbers. Easy, yet impressive.

Ingredients:

      3 large cucumbers - peeled if waxed, otherwise unpeeled, cut in half long ways, with seeds scooped out
      1 lb. firm tofu - mashed
      2 cloves garlic - minced
      1 Tbsp. each - fresh chopped basil, parsley, and dill
      2 Tbsp. balsamic vinegar
      1 Tbsp. lemon juice
      2 green onions - chopped
      1 Tbsp. nutritional yeast/Red Star
      Fresh ground black pepper or cayenne to taste
      Kelp, dulse, or sea salt to taste
      (each will create a new flavor)

Preparation:

Cut each length of cucumber in half, scooping them out and making 6 boats, and set aside. In a large mixing bowl, combine the mashed tofu with all the other ingredients and blend together well. Allow the flavors to marry for a few minutes, then spoon the mixture into the cucumber boats, mounding it on top. Serve on a plate of lettuce, or slice it into 1" pieces and use as party hors d'oeuvres. Garnish with thin pepper slices or tomato wedges. Getting really creative, you can use carrot sticks as masts, pushed through a lettuce leaf for a sail. Kids go wild!!!!

Makes 6 boats

Quick & Easy Fresh Salsa

Ingredients:

> 4-5 medium ripe tomatoes
> 1 green pepper - chopped coarse
> 1 medium onion - chopped coarse
> 1 Tbsp. fresh cilantro/parsley - chopped
> 1 jalapeno pepper - seeded and chopped
>   (use 2 if you like it hot!)
> 1 Tbsp. lemon juice
> 2 cloves garlic - minced/or 1 tsp. granules
> 1 tsp. chili powder (mild)

Preparation:

In a food processor, puree the tomatoes. Add all the other ingredients and pulse until all the veggies are mixed, but not pureed. Serve with your favorite corn chips.

Makes approximately 2 cups

"Fruit bears the closest relationship to light.
The sun pours a continuous flood
of light into the fruits,
and they furnish the best portion of food
a human body requires
for the sustenance of mind and body."

Bronson Alcott

Middle Eastern Kale & Cous Cous Salad

This dish is very simple to make and very nutritious. Most of all, it is deliciously filling!

Ingredients:

 2 lbs. kale - washed, stemmed, and coarsely chopped
 1 Tbsp. canola oil
 1 large onion - chopped
 1/2 cup whole wheat cous cous
 1 cup water
 1/2 lb. dry chickpeas - (soaked overnight, cooked until soft, and drained)
 2 cloves garlic - chopped
 2-3 Tbsp. fresh lemon juice
 Sea salt and fresh ground black pepper to taste

Preparation:

Steam the kale until tender and set aside. In a skillet, heat the oil and sauté the onion and garlic until soft. Add the water, chickpeas, salt, and pepper, and bring to a boil. Stir in the kale and cous cous. Remove from heat and cover for 5 minutes. With a fork, fluff up the cous cous and kale mix and place it on a serving platter or in a bowl. Sprinkle it with the lemon juice. Can be served hot or chilled.

Makes 4 - 6 servings

Green Bean & Chestnut Salad

Coming from Ohio originally, I remember chestnuts fondly. There is no other flavor that can duplicate that of a fresh roasted chestnut. A truly unique salad if I say so myself!

Ingredients:

> 2 10 oz. boxes frozen french cut green beans (thawed, drained, and dried)
> 1 1/2 cups - chestnuts (roasted, shelled and sliced in half)
> 1 Tbsp. sesame oil
> 2 Tbsp. balsamic vinegar
> 3-4 green onions - chopped
> 2 Tbsp. San-J tamari
> 1 Tbsp. canola oil
> 1/4 cup sesame seeds - lightly toasted

Preparation:

Combine the beans and chestnuts in a bowl. In a skillet, heat the canola oil and sauté the onions for 3-5 minutes, or until soft. In a separate bowl, whisk together the sesame oil, vinegar, tamari, and the sautéed onions. Pour over and mix with the beans and nuts. Sprinkle with the sesame seeds and lightly toss, then allow to chill. Can be served as a cold salad on a bed of lettuce, or warmed and served as a hot side dish.

Makes 6 - 8 servings

Spinach & Tofu Salad

For the light lunch or as a salad it's filling and satisfying. Or, if you're like me, just throw it all into a whole wheat tortilla wrap, and eat it on the way to go diving or kayaking. Have fun!

Ingredients:
> 1 lb. raw spinach - washed and drained
> 1 medium red onion
> 1/2 lb. mushrooms - sliced
> 1/4 cup lemon juice
> 1/4 cup water
> 1/4 cup olive oil
> 2 Tbs. San-J tamari
> 2 cloves garlic - minced
> 1 red bell pepper - cut in large pieces
> 1/2 tsp. oregano
> Fresh ground black pepper to taste

Tofu Mix:
> 1 lb. firm tofu - drained well
> 1 Tbsp. garlic powder
> 1 Tbsp. dry basil and parsley
> 1/2 tsp. sea salt
> 1 Tbsp. nutritional yeast/Red Star

Preparation:
In a bowl, combine the spinach, red onion, mushrooms, and pepper, and toss. In a separate bowl, mash the tofu and add the garlic powder, basil, salt, and yeast, and mix thoroughly. Set aside. In a separate bowl, add the lemon, water, oil, tamari, garlic, and oregano, and whisk. Crumble the tofu blend over the spinach mix. Pour whisked dressing on top. Lightly toss and serve.

Makes 4 - 6 servings

North African Bean &
Carrot Salad

I first ate this dish in an Ethiopian restaurant in Washington, D.C. We had so much fun eating all the food with our fingers and the flat bread. You may want to use a fork, but I'm sure you'll too have fun!

Ingredients:

> 2 Tbsp. olive oil
> 1 Tbsp. tahini
> 4 Tbsp. fresh lemon juice
> 1 tsp. cumin
> 4 cups soybeans or white beans (soaked, rinsed, cooked and drained)
> 4 cups carrots - shredded
> 1 large garlic clove - minced
> 2 red bell peppers - julienne cut
> 1 Tbsp. sweet paprika
> 1 cup parsley - chopped
> Sea salt and fresh ground black pepper to taste

Preparation:

In a blender, combine the oil, lemon, tahini, cumin, garlic, paprika, salt, and pepper. In a separate bowl, mix beans, carrots, parsley, and peppers together. Pour the blender mixture over the top and toss well. Allow the ingredients to marry. It is best to plan ahead and let this set overnight.

Makes 8 servings

Quick Slaw

Just what everyone wants to take on their picnic. This American favorite goes great with grain, nut, or soy burgers.

Ingredients:

> 3 carrots - grated
> 1/2 small cabbage - grated
> 2-3 celery stalks - chopped fine
> 2 Tbsp. tofu (non-egg) mayonnaise
> 2 Tbsp. balsamic vinegar
> 2 Tbsp. maple syrup
> 1 Tbsp. San-J tamari

Preparation:

In a large mixing bowl, toss together the carrots, cabbage, and celery. In a separate bowl, whisk the remaining ingredients together. Pour the blend over the veggies and toss again until everything is well coated. Good to make in advance and let the flavors marry. Always tastes better the next day.

Makes 4 - 6 servings

"I do not feel obliged to believe that the same God that has endowed us with sense, reason, and intellect has intended for us to forgo their use."

Galileo

Tofu Russian Mint Relish

While trying to invent a healthy Russian dressing, I happened on this idea, The mint really gives it a whole new taste. I thickened it and now it's a refreshing condiment to add to your table.

Ingredients:

>1/2 lb. tofu - soft or silken
>4 cups tomatoes - chopped
>2 tsp. fresh mint - diced fine
>1/2 cup fructose or sweetener
>1 cup red wine vinegar - divided into 2 halves
>1 red onion - chopped
>1/2 cup cucumbers - peeled and diced
>1 tsp. ground cumin
>1 tsp. ground coriander
>2 garlic cloves - minced
>Salt and pepper to taste
>1 tsp. grated fresh ginger

Preparation:

Add everything, except the tofu, 1/2 the vinegar, and the cucumbers in a saucepan, and bring to a boil. Reduce heat and simmer, covered, for 20 minutes. In a blender, add the tofu and the remaining 1/2 cup of vinegar together and blend until smooth. Pulse in the cucumbers, being careful not to chop them up to much. Combine the tofu blend and add to the saucepan after the 20 minutes. Stir everything together. Simmer uncovered for 10 more minutes, stirring frequently. Allow to cool slightly and serve over grain loaf or fresh greens.

Note: If you don't have fresh mint, you can use 1 tsp. of dried mint in its place.

Makes approximately 2 1/2 - 3 servings

Tofu Wild Rice Salad

The distinctive taste of the wild rice lends its flavor for this dish. Light, as well as low in fat; a pleasing blend for any meal.

Ingredients:

1/2 lb. firm tofu - drained well
1 small zucchini - grated
1 carrot - grated
2 green onions - chopped
1 red bell pepper - cut in 2" strips
1/2 cup **Lundberg** wild rice
1/2 cup **Lundberg** brown rice (long grain)
2 cups water
1/4 tsp. sea salt

Dressing:

2 Tbsp. olive oil
2 Tbsp. miso
3 Tbsp. balsamic vinegar
1/2 tsp. each - basil, thyme, and sage
Cayenne or fresh ground black pepper to taste

Marinade:

2 Tbsp. San-J tamari
2 Tbsp. water
1/2 tsp. garlic powder
1 Tbsp. fresh grated ginger

Preparation:
In a mixing bowl, combine the marinade ingredients together. Cube the tofu, place in a shallow dish, and cover it with the marinade. Let it sit for at least 2 hours, turning several times. In a saucepan, bring the water and salt to a boil. Add the rice and cook until all the water has been absorbed, (approximately 50-60 minutes). Allow it to cool. In a mixing bowl, combine all the dressing ingredients together and whisk well. Toss the rice with the rest of the ingredients, except the tofu and the dressing. Pour the dressing over the tofu, then pour everything over the rice mix. Toss gently, but thoroughly, and chill. Can be served warm as well.

Makes 4 servings

"From an early age I have abjured the use of meat,
and the time will come when men will look
upon the murder of animals
as they look upon the murder of men."

Leonardo Da Vinci

Greek Salad

Here's a twist on an old familiar dish. Instead of the Feta cheese, we use tofu and spices.

Ingredients:
>4 red bell peppers - roasted *
>2 green bell peppers - chopped
>1 large onion - chopped
>1/2 lb. firm tofu - crumbled
>1/2 cup olive oil
>1 cup Greek olives (salty, wrinkled ones)
>1 cup green olives - pitted
>3 Tbsp. lemon juice
>1/2 tsp. each - salt, oregano, and dill
>2-3 cloves garlic - minced
>Romaine lettuce (washed and torn) for 6
>Fresh ground black pepper to taste.
>Fresh parsley for garnish

Preparation:
*Roast the peppers by holding them over a flame until the skins blister and turn black. Rinse under cold water, removing the blackened skin. Remove seeds and cut into medium squares. Combine the oil, lemon, garlic, oregano, dill, and salt, and whisk well. In a marinade dish, combine the crumbled tofu and onion. Pour marinade on top and toss well. Refrigerate and allow to marinate at least 2 hours.

To serve, place the lettuce on a platter or a salad bowl. Mix in the green pepper and green olives. Spoon on the marinated tofu. Cover with the roasted red peppers and Greek olives, and garnish with pepper and fresh parsley.

Makes 6 servings

Caesar Salad

Replace the egg and cheese with healthy substitutes for vegans!

Ingredients*:*
> 2 Romaine lettuce heads - washed and torn
> 4 green onions - chopped
> 1 cup imitation bacon bits - vegetarian
> 1 cup croutons/toasted bread pieces
> 1/2 lb. firm tofu - crumbled
> 1 tsp. turmeric
> 2 tsp. San-J tamari
> 1 Tbsp. canola oil
> Fresh ground black pepper garnish

Dressing:
> 1/2 cup olive oil
> 5-6 Tbsp. lemon juice
> 2 cloves garlic - crushed
> 1 Tbsp. tahini
> 2 Tbsp. nutritional yeast/Red Star
> 3/4 tsp. sea salt
> 1/2 tsp. dried mint & fresh ground black pepper

Preparation:
In a bowl, combine the tofu, tamari, and turmeric. In a skillet, heat a Tbsp. of cooking oil and add the tofu mix. Cook for several minutes on one side and flip. Allow to lightly brown, then scramble the tofu up, and remove from heat and cool. Mix lettuce, onions, imitation bacon, and tofu scramble all together. In a separate bowl, whisk all the dressing ingredients together. Pour over the salad and toss well. Add the croutons and lightly toss again.
Note: To avoid a soggy salad, don't dress the salad until just before you are ready to serve it.

Makes 8 or more servings

Tofu Eggless Salad

Tofu eggless salad makes great sandwiches. Or you can stuff it into mushroom caps, put it under the grill until browned, and you've got "Eggless Angels," instead of Deviled Eggs!

Ingredients:
>1 lb. firm tofu - crumbled
>2 stalks of celery - diced
>1 red bell pepper - chopped
>4 green onions - chopped
>1 tsp. garlic powder
>2 Tbsp. San-J tamari
>1 tsp. turmeric
>Cayenne or fresh black pepper to taste

Preparation:
In a mixing bowl, combine all the ingredients well, but don't beat it smooth. Serve it on bread or stuff a tomato. Either way it's great and cholesterol free!

Makes 4 servings

*"The ideals which have lighted my way,
and time after time have given me new courage
to face life cheerfully,
have been kindness, beauty, and truth."*

Albert Einstein

Marinated Stuffed Avocados

Lets face it. If you love avocados, you can eat them in any way, shape, or form. This is a very delicious variation that everyone is bound to enjoy.

Ingredients:

> 2 medium/large avocados
> 1 medium onion - chopped
> 1/2 cup mushrooms - chopped
> 1 red bell pepper - seeded and chopped
> 3-4 Tbsp. San-J tamari
> 2 Tbsp. balsamic vinegar
> 1 Tbsp. nutritional yeast/Red Star
> 1/2 tsp. garlic powder
> Cayenne or fresh black pepper to taste
> 1/4 cup roasted sunflower or sesame seeds

Preparation:

In a skillet over medium heat, roast the sunflower/sesame seeds, turning frequently until browned. (They will pop when roasted.) Set aside. Slice the avocados in half, remove the pit, and carefully scrape out the insides into a mixing bowl. Save the shells and set aside. Combine the avocado with all the other ingredients, except the sunflower or sesame seeds, and stir well until creamy. Spoon the filling back into the shells. Mound them up, or make a pita sandwich for the chef with the overflow, and sprinkle with the sunflower/sesame seeds. Refrigerate at least 2 hours. Bring to room temperature before serving.

Makes 4 servings

Bean Salad with Cucumber Dressing

This dish looks as good as it tastes. If you want to impress your guests, this will score high. Good for large parties as well, because it's inexpensive, easy to make, and quick to assemble.

Ingredients:

2 cups dry soy beans (soaked overnight, rinsed well and drained)

1/2 cup dry chickpeas (soaked overnight, rinsed well, and drained)

1/2 cup red kidney beans (soaked overnight, rinsed well, and drained)

1 small green bell pepper - chopped

2 large tomatoes - chopped

1 large celery stalk - chopped fine

1 small onion - chopped

4 Tbsp. San-J tamari

1/2 tsp. ginger powder

2 carrots - grated

1 large cucumber - peeled, seeded, and chopped

1 Tbsp. cider vinegar

1 tsp. fresh dill

1 tsp. Dijon mustard

Sea salt and pepper to taste

2 Tbsp. lemon juice

Enough mixed greens for 6 people

Preparation:
Boil the soaked beans until tender (approximately 1 hour). 1 minute before completion, add the green pepper and blanch for one minute. Rinse with cold water, and drain. Add the tomatoes, celery, onion, 2 Tbsp. tamari, lemon juice, and ginger, and toss well. Set aside.

In a blender, combine the cucumber, vinegar, 2 Tbsp. tamari, mustard, dill, water (if necessary), and salt and pepper to taste. Blend well. To serve, place a salad size portion of greens on a plate, sprinkle with the grated carrot, spoon 3-4 Tbsp. of bean mix on top and spread it out a little. Surround the beans with the cucumber dressing. Garnish and serve.

Makes 6 servings

*"The earth I tread on is not dead, inert mass.
It is a body, has a spirit, is organic,
and fluid to the influence of its spirit,
and to whatever particle of that spirit
is in me."*

Henry David Thoreau

Hot or Cold Green Beans with Tofu Green Onion Sauce

Ingredients:

    1 lb. green beans - cleaned and stemmed
    5-6 green onions - chopped
    3 garlic cloves - chopped
    2 Tbsp. lemon juice
    1 Tbsp. prepared mustard
    1 tsp. sea salt or 2 Tbsp. San-J tamari
    Cayenne or black pepper to taste
    1/2 cup red pepper (sweet) - chopped
    1/3 lb. or 1/2 a box of silken tofu
      (or soft tofu with a Tbsp. of water)

Preparation:

Steam green beans until just tender, but still firm. (If serving as a cold salad, rinse and chill the beans at this point.) Drain and toss with the red peppers. Set aside.

Reserve some of the green onion tops for a garnish. Place all the remaining ingredients in a blender or processor. Blend everything until creamy smooth. (In the blender a little extra water may be needed.)

Pour over the hot beans and serve immediately. Or you can chill it and serve it on a bed of greens with tomato wedges, topped with a generous helping of the tofu/onion cream. Garnish either style with green onion tops.

Makes 4 - 6 servings

European Tofu Potato & Beet Salad

Ingredients:

- 1 1/2 cups beets - peeled and cubed
- 2 cups potatoes - scrubbed and cubed (peeling optional)
- 1 cucumber peeled, seeded and cubed
- 2 celery stalks - chopped
- 1 onion - chopped
- 1/2 lb. silken tofu
- 2 Tbsp. prepared mustard
- 1 Tbsp. San-J tamari
- 1 Tbsp. unrefined sweetener (i.e., beet sugar, date sugar, etc.)
- 2 Tbsp. fresh dill
- Pepper to taste (black and cayenne)
- Enough water to blend tofu with

Preparation:

In a large pot, steam the potatoes and beets until they're just becoming tender (check the centers with knives or toothpicks). Add the chopped onion and steam for 2 more minutes. Rinse with cold water and drain. Toss lightly with the cucumber, green onion, and celery, and set aside.

In a blender, combine all the remaining ingredients. Blend until smooth and creamy. Pour the tofu blend over the veggie mix and toss gently, but thoroughly. Allow some time to chill slightly and for the flavors to marry. Garnish with fresh parsley and serve on a bed of your favorite greens.

Makes 4 - 6 servings

Spinach Salad with
Poppy Seed Dressing

The light sweet taste of the dressing lends to the flavor of the spinach. A beautiful low fat lunch for anytime or season.

Ingredients:

1 lb. fresh spinach - washed and torn
1/2 lb. mushrooms - sliced
1 cup water chestnuts - sliced
1 large red onion - sliced thin
2 carrots - grated
1 cup croutons/toasted bread pieces

Dressing:

1/2 cup canola oil
5-6 Tbsp. balsamic vinegar
1 tsp. poppy seeds
1 Tbsp. onion - chopped
1/2 cup maple syrup/sweetener
3/4 tsp. dry mustard
3/4 tsp. sea salt

Preparation:

In a salad bowl, combine and toss all the ingredients, except for the dressing ingredients and croutons. In a blender, combine all the dressing ingredients, except the poppy seeds, and blend until smooth. Add the poppy seeds and pulse in. Pour the dressing over the salad, sprinkle with the croutons, toss and serve.

Makes 6 - 8 servings

Roasted Tomato & Tofu Salad

This Mediterranean dish goes well as an antipasto or side dish with any Italian or Greek meal. Try it with fresh bread or pizza.

Ingredients:

1 Tbsp. sesame oil
2 Tbsp. San-J tamari
1 lb. firm tofu - drained and cubed
4 large ripe tomatoes
1 Tbsp. lime juice
2 Tbsp. maple syrup
1 tsp. jalapeno or chili pepper - minced
1/2 tsp. each - oregano, thyme, cumin, and
   coriander
2 cloves of garlic - minced
1 Tbsp. apple cider vinegar
Pinch of sea salt (optional)
1 Tbsp. fresh parsley chopped
1 tsp. sesame seeds

Preparation:

Heat the oil and add the tofu cubes. Sauté for several minutes. Add the tamari and continue to sauté until all the moisture has been absorbed and the tofu is lightly grilled. Remove, cool, and set aside. On a skewer, directly hold each of the tomatoes over an open gas flame, turning until the skin becomes charred and blistered. Let cool, hold under cold water, then carefully peel off the skin and dice the remaining tomatoes. In a mixing bowl, combine all the remaining ingredients and mix well. Pour over the tofu, garnish with the parsley and sesame seeds, and lightly chill. Serve on a bed of lettuce or fresh spinach.

Makes 6 - 8 servings

Dressings
and
Sauces

Tamari Glaze

This is good to change any plain dish or veggie into something new and different. Change the spices and you change the glaze.

Ingredients:
- 1 cup San-J tamari
- 1 1/2 cup water
- 3 Tbsp. arrowroot
- 1 tsp. garlic powder
- 1 Tbsp. nutritional yeast/Red Star

Preparation:
Combine all the ingredients well. In a saucepan, over medium heat, stir constantly until it thickens. Remove it from the stove and serve.

Lychee & Ginger Sauce

Ingredients:
- 2 cups lychees - peeled and seeded/or canned
- 1 Tbsp. fresh grated ginger
- 1 Tbsp. lemon juice
- 1 Tbsp. mirin

Preparation:
In a blender, combine all the ingredients and blend until smooth. Can be used over Nice Dream (page 193) or your favorite cakes, pastries, or muffins.

Makes approximately 2 cups

Brown Gravy

There are so many ways to make brown gravy, but this has a nice rich savory taste to it. Use your own special flare and make your own favorite.

Ingredients:

4 cups water
4 Tbsp. whole wheat flour
2 Tbsp. nutritional yeast/Red Star
1/4 cup Bragg's liquid amino or vegetable soup stock cube
1 tsp. onion powder
1/2 tsp. thyme
Pinch of salt and pepper

Preparation:

Mix all the ingredients together and heat over a medium fire, stirring regularly until the gravy thickens. Use over your favorite grain or pasta.

Makes approximately 1 quart

*"A man is truly ethical only when he obeys
the compulsion to help all life,
which he is able to assist,
and shrinks from injuring anything that lives."*

Albert Schweitzer

Lemon & Basil White Sauce

This sauce has a lighter taste to it then the regular white sauce, due to the arrowroot powder in place of the flour. It goes especially nice over steamed veggies, grain dishes, or one of the many sea vegetable dishes you can make. I make a dish with seitan (wheat gluten meat), where I flavor it with kelp and dulse, and get a fake fish taste. With this sauce it's like an imitation "filet of sole".

Ingredients:
    1 cup soy milk or nut milk
    2 Tbsp. lemon juice
    1 Tbsp. arrowroot powder
    2 Tbsp. canola oil (optional)
    2 Tbsp. fresh basil - chopped fine
    Sea salt and white pepper to taste

Preparation:
In a saucepan, combine all the ingredients except the basil and lemon juice, and place over a medium heat, stirring constantly. When the sauce thickens, add the lemon and basil, and stir well. Remove from heat. Pour over pasta, grains, or steamed veggies.

Makes approximately 1 cup

"Out of clutter find simplicity.
From discord, find harmony.
In the middle of difficulty lies opportunity."

Albert Einstein

Creamy Onion Sauce

This is great either poured over fresh or steamed veggies, or used in a casserole or grain dish. Easy and quick to make, too!

Ingredients:
>   1/2 lb. soft tofu
>   1/3 cup soy or nut milk
>   1 large onion - chopped
>   2 green onions - chopped
>   1 Tbsp. canola oil
>   1 Tbsp. San-J tamari
>   2 tsp. dry parsley
>   1/2 tsp. each - basil and paprika
>   Sea salt and fresh ground black pepper to taste
>   Cayenne pepper to taste

Preparation:
Heat the oil and sauté the onion for 3 minutes. Combine the sauté and the rest of the ingredients, except green onions, in a blender, and blend until smooth. Pour into a medium sauce pan and heat over a medium/low fire. DO NOT BOIL! Stir in the green onions and serve over your favorite pasta, grain, or veggies.

Makes approximately 1 cup

"The truth is much more important than the facts."

Frank Lloyd Wright

Parsnip &
Ginger Tofu White Sauce

Parsnips have a beautiful light sweet taste. I've tried to take that flavor, and combine it in a creamy sauce. It's marvelous over fresh greens, or potato chunks.

Ingredients:
1 cup parsnips - peeled and diced
1 medium onion - chopped
1 Tbsp. fresh grated ginger
1 1/2 cups water
Sea salt and fresh ground black pepper to taste
1/4 lb. soft tofu

Preparation:
In a saucepan, put the water, salt and pepper, ginger, onion, and parsnips, on a medium heat. Cover and cook until the parsnips are tender, about 10-15 minutes. Place everything in a blender and add the tofu. Blend until smooth. Adjust the seasonings and pour over your favorite grains or veggies.

Makes approximately 2 1/2 cups

"We have it in our power to begin the earth again."

Thomas Paine

Tofu French Onion & Mustard Sauce

Now this is a tasty sauce. I love to pour this one over fresh steamed asparagus or broccoli. Very rich and creamy, just like the French love it (only without the cholesterol!). Oui!

Ingredients:

1 lb. soft or silken tofu
1/2 cup fresh fennel - chopped
2 Tbsp. Dijon mustard
1 tsp. fresh tarragon
2 medium onions - chopped
1 Tbsp. canola oil
Sea salt and fresh pepper to taste

Preparation:

In a skillet, heat the oil and sauté the onions and fennel for 3-5 minutes until the onions are translucent. In a food processor, add all the ingredients including the onions and fennel, and process until smooth, about 45 seconds to 1 minute. Pour over the steamed broccoli or asparagus, or serve over your favorite grain. Chill it, add a little water, blend, and use it as a salad dressing.

Makes approximately 2 cups

"One word frees us of all the weight and pain of life;
That word is love."

Sophocles

Basic Creamy White Sauce

In Italy I discovered when you don't want a red sauce, they give you a white cream sauce. Trouble is, it's loaded with animal fat and cholesterol. Using soy milk or nut milk cuts most of the saturated fat and all of the cholesterol out, while still leaving in the rich flavor. Spice it as you like and enjoy.

Ingredients:

> 2 Tbsp. unbleached flour
> 1 tsp. oil (canola/olive)
> 1 1/2 cups of pine nut milk/soy milk
> 2-3 cloves garlic - minced
> Sea salt and fresh ground white pepper to taste
> 3-4 Tbsp. fresh parsley - chopped fine

Preparation:

Over low heat, lightly dry roast the flour, stirring constantly, for several minutes. Add everything but the parsley and continue to stir until the sauce thickens. Remove from the heat and stir in the parsley. Serve over fresh steamed veggies or your favorite pasta.

Makes 3 - 4 servings

*"A moment's insight is sometimes worth
a life's experience."*

Oliver Wendell Holmes Sr.

Barbecue Sauce

A simple "do it yourself" sauce. Saves you from running out to the store every time you need some. And a whole lot cheaper this way too!

Ingredients:

> 1/2 cup sweetener of your choice (like maple syrup)
> 1 15 oz. can tomato sauce
> 1 large can tomato paste
> 1/8 cup cider vinegar
> 3 tsp. chili powder (less for milder sauce)
> 1/8 tsp. mild cayenne pepper (optional)
> 1/2 tsp. onion powder
> Pinch of salt
> Water as needed to bring to your desired consistency

Preparation:

Combine all the ingredients together well. Keep the remainder in the refrigerator until needed.

Variations and different tastes make possibilities almost unlimited!

Makes approximately 1 quart

Tangy Tomato Dressing

A nice change of pace from the normal oil & vinegar, or tahini type dressings. Good for when you have a lot of ripe tomatoes and don't want to make sauce out of all of them.

Ingredients:

> 1 1/2 cups tomatoes - seeded and chopped
> 1/2 cup olive or flaxseed oil
> 1/2 small onion - chopped
> 1-2 Tbsp. apple cider vinegar
> 1-2 Tbsp. maple syrup
> 1/2 tsp. each - basil, garlic powder, and kelp
> Sea salt and fresh ground black pepper to taste

Preparation:

In a blender, combine all the ingredients together and blend until smooth. Chill and serve.

Makes approximately 2 cups

"All love is sweet, given or returned.
They who inspire it most are fortunate,
but those who feel it most
are happier still."

Percy Bysshe Shelly

Tofu Tahini/Lemon Dressing

The old standard, except I like to use tofu to thicken it. Makes it a little more rich and creamy, without disturbing the taste that you've grown to enjoy.

Ingredients:
>1 cup soft tofu
>1/2 cup tahini
>1/2 - 1 cup water, as needed to thin
>1/8 cup canola oil optional (just use less water)
>1/2 cup fresh lemon juice
>1/2 small onion - chopped
>1 Tbsp. dry parsley
>Sea salt, cayenne, and black pepper to taste

Preparation:
In a blender, combine all the ingredients until smooth. You can either use it immediately as a sauce for your favorite grain, or chill and enjoy it with a beautiful garden salad.

Makes approximately 3 1/2 cups

"To a man with an empty stomach, food is god."

Mahatma Gandhi

Lemon, Basil & Herb Dressing

This is great if you have your own garden and can pick the fresh herbs fresh just before using (dried or packaged herbs will do, but fresh is best). You can vary your herbs for different taste combinations too.

Ingredients:
1 cup canola oil
1 Tbsp. fresh basil - chopped
4-5 Tbsp. fresh lemon juice
1 Tbsp. dry parsley
1 tsp. sea salt
1/2 tsp. each - fresh thyme and oregano
1/4 tsp. each - ground sage and ground rosemary
1 tsp. nutritional yeast/Red Star
Cayenne or ground black pepper to taste

Preparation:
In a blender, combine all the ingredients and blend until smooth. Allow ample time for the flavors to marry, and use or chill. Shake well before using.

Makes approximately 1 1/4 cups

"This above all: to thine own self be true,
and it must follow, as the night to the day,
thou canst not be false to any man."

William Shakespeare

Creamy Cucumber Dill Dressing

Kind of like eating an un-pickle! A several thousand year old combination can't be wrong. I've heard that pregnant women love this dressing. (They just eat it over their "Nice Dream" instead!)

Ingredients:

1 cup soft or silken tofu
1 large cucumber - peeled, seeded, and chopped
1/4 cup flaxseed oil or olive oil
1/8 - 1/4 cup water - as needed
1 Tbsp. fresh dill - chopped
1/4 tsp. kelp
1 green onion - chopped
Sea salt and fresh ground black pepper to taste
Cayenne pepper to taste - optional

Preparation:

In a blender, combine all the ingredients and blend until smooth. Chill and serve. Can be refrigerated for 3-4 days.

Makes 2 1/2 - 3 cups

"Human kindness has never weakened the stamina or softened the fiber of a free people. A nation does not have to be cruel to be tough."

Franklin D. Roosevelt

Creamy Miso Dressing

This is my favorite dressing. I just love this on top of a great big spinach salad. It's a whole meal for me. Use this on your grain dishes as well, or as a sauce for your pita sandwiches.

Ingredients:

      2 cups soft or silken tofu
      1/8 cup cider vinegar
      2 Tbsp. lemon juice
      1 Tbsp. prepared mustard
      2 Tbsp. white/yellow miso
      1/8 cup Mirin (or sweetener)
      Water if needed

Preparation:

Combine all the ingredients in a blender and blend until smooth. Serve over your favorite salad, greens, or grain of choice.

Makes approximately 2 1/2 cups

*"The true light is that which emanates
from within man,
and reveals the secrets of the heart to the soul,
making it happy, and contented with life."*

Kahlil Gibran

Papaya Seed Dressing

Living in Hawaii gave me access to so many wonderful foods, but the healthiest one of all I think, must be the papaya. A wonderfully sweet fruit that contains a center filled with hundreds of small round black seeds. Great for the digestion, and at the same time, so delicious.

Ingredients:

    1 Tbsp. papaya seeds (washed and dried)
    1/4 cup rice vinegar
    1/2 small onion - chopped
    2 Tbsp. maple syrup/sweetener
    1/4 tsp. sea salt
    1 tsp. prepared mustard
    1/2 cup canola oil

Preparation:

In a blender, chop the papaya seeds until coarse. Add the vinegar and blend. Combine the rest of the ingredients. Blend until creamy. Serve over greens or fruit salad.

Makes approximately one cup

*"When it breathes through his intellect,
it is genius.
When it breathes through his will,
it is virtue.
When it flows through his affection,
it is love."*

Ralph Waldo Emerson

Spreads
&
Dips

"The quantity of nutritious vegetable matter
consumed in fattening the carcass of an ox,
would afford ten times the sustenance
undepraving indeed, and incapable
of generating disease,
if gathered immediately from the bosom of the earth.
The most fertile districts of the inhabitable globe
are now actually cultivated by men for animals,
at a delay and waste of aliment
absolutely incapable of calculation.
It is only the wealthy that can,
to any great degree, even now,
indulge the unnatural craving for dead flesh,
and they pay for the greater license of the privilege
by subjection to supernumerary diseases."

Percy Bysshe Shelley

Soybean Spread

People are always asking me which is better, margarine or butter. My response is, "I wouldn't use either of them." They are both sources of saturated fat. If a teaspoon of flaxseed oil doesn't appeal to you, try this creamy topping - the perfect butter spread replacement. Use this on toast in the morning, or to make your garlic bread at night.

Ingredients:

4 cups soybeans (soaked, cooked, and drained)
3 cloves garlic - diced
1 small onion - chopped
1/2 cup olive oil
2 Tbsp. lemon juice
1 tsp. sea salt
Water if needed

Preparation:

In a food processor, blend all the ingredients together until smooth. Refrigerate and use on your favorite "French Meadow" breads for your toast in the morning, or as a sandwich spread on your favorite biscuits or bagels.

Makes about 4 1/2 cups

"The love we give away is the only love we keep."

Elbert Green Hubbard

French Olive Spread

In the old days, I could see eating this on a picnic, by a stream, with a nice sour dough bread, and a bottle of red wine. Now I still enjoy it, but I drink alcohol-free wine. Not very French of me, though. Just like the French to have these terribly rich spreads. Lucky for us, the cholesterol worries don't have to go along with the calorie ones. So enjoy it to your heart's content. (I mean that literally!)

Ingredients:

> 1 cup pitted black olives (salty Greek or Provencal)
> 1/2 cup firm tofu - well drained
> 2 garlic cloves - minced
> 1 Tbsp. olive oil
> 2 Tbsp. capers
> 2 tbsp. lemon juice
> 1 tsp. Dijon prepared mustard
> 1/2 tsp. each - thyme, rosemary, and parsley
> Fresh ground black pepper to taste

Preparation:

In a bowl, mash the tofu, olives, and capers together well. Add the rest of the ingredients and mix together thoroughly. Chill and serve on toasted triangles of "French Meadow's" rye and sunflower seed bread as an hors d'oeuvre.

Makes approximately 1 1/2 cups of spread

Fresh Garlic Spread

The garlic lover's ultimate delight. Guaranteed not to have any problems with vampires!

Ingredients:
>   20-25 garlic cloves
>   1/2 cup firm tofu - drained well
>   1 Tbsp. olive oil
>   1/4 tsp. each - dried basil, thyme, and rosemary
>   Sea salt and fresh ground black pepper to taste

Preparation:
In a small casserole dish, place the garlic, oil, and herbs. Stir well and bake covered in a 350° oven for 40-50 minutes. Place in a processor with the tofu and blend until smooth. Add the salt and pepper to taste and serve on your favorite bread or pasta. Use instead of butter. Keeps about 3-5 days refrigerated.

Makes approximately 3/4 cup

*"Happiness makes up in height
for what it lacks in length."*

Robert Frost

Vegan Cheeses

Revolutionary is all I can say! I thought for sure I'd given up (or down as the case may be) cheese forever. I understood the bad health and ethical aspects of dairy, but still admit I reminisced about the taste. I give credit for the original idea of using oats as the coagulant to Joanne Stepaniak and her "Uncheese Cookbook", which I highly recommend. Now try this on your pizza or lasagna, smile, and say, "Cheese!"

Ingredients:

'Moats-erella':
- 1 cup rolled oats
- 4 Tbsp. tahini
- 4 Tbsp. arrowroot powder (or 2 Tbsp. for pourable toppings like pizza & lasagna)
- 1 tsp. onion powder
- 1 tsp. sea salt
- 3 Tbsp. nutritional yeast/Red Star
- 3 Tbsp. lemon juice
- 2 cups water

Gruyere:
- 1 cup rolled oats
- 3 Tbsp. tahini
- 4 Tbsp. arrowroot
- 2 tsp. onion powder
- 1/2 tsp. sea salt
- 4 Tbsp. nutritional yeast/Red Star
- 4 Tbsp. lemon juice
- 2 cups water

Preparation:
Place all the ingredients of your choice of cheese in a blender and blend until smooth. In a saucepan, over medium heat, pour the blend in and stir constantly for approximately 2 minutes, or until the mixture becomes thick but will still pour. You can remove it at that point, or continue to cook it to a solid form, stirring constantly until it balls up and separates from the sides of the pot. (Stir very fast at the end for the smoothest consistency.) Use immediately as a topping if in liquid form (like for pizza or parmesan) or place the thicker portion in a lightly oiled mold and chill into a solid form. Can be used as a spread, or sliced carefully with a clean, wet knife.

Makes approximately 1 lb. of vegan cheese.

*"Man can no longer live for himself alone.
We must realize that all life is valuable
and that we are united to all life.
From this knowledge
comes our spiritual relationship
with the universe."*

Albert Schweitzer

Balsamic Cheesy Spread

I discovered this one night when I went to make my "Moatsarella" cheese and didn't have any lemon juice. We were pleasantly surprised—and I'm sure you'll agree!

Ingredients:

> 1 cup rolled oats
> 4 Tbsp. balsamic vinegar
> 1/2 small onion - chopped
> 3 Tbsp. arrowroot powder
> 1/4 cup nutritional yeast/Red Star
> 3 Tbsp. tahini
> 1/2 tsp. fresh ground black pepper
> 1 1/2 cups water
> 1 Tbsp. San-J tamari

Preparation:

Combine all the ingredients in a blender and blend until smooth. Over medium heat, pour the blend into a saucepan and stir constantly for about 2 minutes. The mixture will thicken. Continue to stir until totally congealed. Remove from the heat and use immediately, or place in a lightly oiled container or mold, and refrigerate. Makes a great spread for crackers or rice cakes.

Makes approximately 2 1/2 cups

*"Life is what happens to us
while we're making other plans."*

John Lennon

Olive & Black Bean Dip

This Spanish style dip is a favorite at parties. Roll it up in your favorite wrap (i.e. tortilla, chapati, flat bread, etc.) along with fresh lettuce and sprouts, or veggies of your choice, and make a delicious lunch treat or snack.

Ingredients:

2 cups black beans (soaked, cooked, and drained)
3/4 - 1 cup pitted black olives
1 medium onion - chopped
1/2 green bell pepper - chopped
1-2 jalapeno peppers - seeded and diced (make
    hotness to your desired taste)
3 cloves garlic - minced
2 Tbsp. cider vinegar
1 tsp. turmeric
2 Tbsp. fresh cilantro
1 tsp. oregano
Sea salt and fresh ground black pepper to taste
2 Tbsp. water and 1 Tbsp. San-J tamari
    or 1 Tbsp. oil

Preparation:

In a skillet, heat the tamari and water, and lightly sauté the onions and garlic. Add the sauté and the rest of the ingredients together and place in a food processor. Puree the mixture until it's smooth, adding additional water if needed to attain the right consistency. Adjust your spices and serve with your favorite chips or fresh veggies.

Makes 4 - 6 servings

Tofu, Spinach & Pine Nut Dip

This is one of my personal favorites. Adapted from one of my relative's'recipes, it makes a great dip or snack. I can eat a whole head of broccoli just dipping it in this and watching a good movie.

Ingredients:

> 12 oz. frozen chopped spinach (thawed and drained)
> 1/2 lb. soft tofu - drained
> 1/2 cup pine nuts - roasted
> 1 Tbsp. San-J tamari
> 1 medium onion - chopped
> 2 cloves garlic - minced
> 1 Tbsp. canola oil
> Cayenne or fresh ground black pepper to taste

Preparation:

In a skillet, heat the oil and sauté the onion and garlic for 2-3 minutes. Remove it from heat. In a food processor, combine the sauté with the remaining ingredients and blend until smooth. Pour over the steamed vegetables as is, or chill and use it as a cold dip with your favorite crackers or fresh-cut veggies.

Makes 4 - 6 servings

"The art of medicine consists in amusing the patient while nature cures the disease."

Voltaire

Chickpea Lime Spread

*Very similar to hummus, and yet, a different taste altogether.
Came upon this through an error. I thought I was putting in lemon
juice, and it turned out to be lime. I wonder if that's how Edison
did it, too.*

Ingredients:

2 cups chickpeas (soaked, cooked, and drained)
1 Tbsp. tahini
1 medium lime - juiced
1 Tbsp. San-J tamari
1 Tbsp. nutritional yeast/Red Star
1/2 tsp. garlic powder
1 small onion - chopped
3-4 Tbsp. water
1/8 cup fresh parsley - chopped
Cayenne pepper to taste

Preparation:

In a mixing bowl, mash the chickpeas. In a separate bowl,
combine all the remaining ingredients except the onions
and parsley, and blend or whisk. Mix the onions and the
parsley in with the chickpeas, then pour the liquid part in
and stir thoroughly. Allow to sit for a few minutes so the
flavors will marry, then serve. Goes great on French bread,
with a bowl of onion soup.

Makes 4 servings

Spicy Bean Dip

This is one of my favorite snacks. When you're hungry and nothing is made, this can be prepared in minutes. Eat it with celery sticks or your favorite low-fat chips. This is also a great low-fat, high protein dish. Goes superb with salsa and rice.

Ingredients:

> 4 cups pinto/red/or navy beans (soaked, cooked and drained)
> 1/2 cup tomato sauce
> 3-4 cloves garlic - minced
> 2 Tbsp. San-J tamari
> 1-2 jalapeno peppers - seeded and diced (to your desired hotness)
> 1/2 tsp. each - oregano, basil, and parsley
> 3 green onions - chopped (save a few of the green chives for garnish)

Preparation:

Combine all the ingredients, except the garnish, in a food processor. Blend to your desired consistency, adding water if needed. Garnish it with green onions and serve.

Makes 6 - 8 servings

*"Every animal that walks the earth,
or swims, or flies is precious beyond description,
something so rare and wonderful that it equals
the stars or the ocean or the mind of man."*

James A. Michener

Tofu Pistachio/Olive Dip

This one is for the non-dieters. Place this out at your party and watch it disappear faster than anything else. Use sliced zucchini instead of chips for an outrageous combination!

Ingredients:
>1 lb. firm tofu
>1/2 cup green olives - with pimentos
>1/2 cup black olives - pitted
>1/4 cup lemon juice
>1/2 tsp. sea salt
>2 Tbsp. olive oil
>1 cup pistachios - shelled
>2 Tbsp. water
>2 Tbsp. chives or green onion tops - chopped
>1 tsp. sweet paprika

Preparation:
Process the nuts to a fine meal. Combine all the remaining ingredients, except the chives and paprika, in a food processor and blend until smooth. Stir in the chives and sprinkle with the paprika. Chill and serve.

Note: This can also be served hot as a sauce as well. Just thin it a little with water and heat it. Goes great on asparagus or green beans. Use it over your favorite pasta.

Makes approximately 4 cups

Pinto Bean, Garlic & Vinegar Dip

A little planning is necessary to remember to soak the beans ahead of time here. This high protein dip goes great on celery as an appetizer, or on your favorite cracker or rice cake.

Ingredients:

- 1 cup dry pinto beans (soaked overnight, drained and rinsed)
- 3 Tbsp. San-J tamari
- 1/8 cup rice vinegar
- 3 cloves garlic - minced
- 2 Tbsp. olive oil
- 1 tsp. dry sweet basil
- 3 Tbsp. nutritional yeast/Red Star
- 1 small onion - chopped
- Cayenne or black pepper to taste
- 2-3 bay leaves
- Sliced tomatoes & Italian parsley for garnish

Preparation:

In a pot, cover the beans with water and bring to a boil. Add bay leaves and simmer for 35-40 minutes or until beans are tender. Drain and rinse in cold water. Remove and compost the bay leaves. In a food processor, combine the beans with the remaining ingredients and puree until almost smooth. (Add a drop of water if needed.) Garnish with the tomatoes and Italian parsley. Use as a sandwich spread or as a chip dip.

Makes 6 - 8 servings

Tofu Horseradish Dip

As a kid I used to grate the horseradish root, until my eyes watered and burned. Later in life, I used to love creamy horseradish. Now, I've found a delightful way of putting the two tastes together. Try it, you'll like it!

Ingredients:
>   1 lb. soft tofu - rinsed
>   1/8 cup rice vinegar
>   1/4 cup horseradish root - peeled and chopped
>   2 green onions - coarsely chopped
>   2 Tbsp. fresh parsley
>   Sea salt and fresh black pepper to taste

Preparation:
In a food processor, put the horseradish chunks in, and grate them until fine. Add the rest of the ingredients and blend until smooth (about 1 minute). Pour into a bowl and serve. It also goes well served over seitan as a sauce, or served over cucumbers as a side dish or salad.

Makes approximately 2 1/2 cups

*"A wise man should consider that health
is the greatest of human blessings,
and learn how by his own thought
to derive benefit from his illness."*

Hippocrates

Roasted Eggplant & Mint Dip

The tofu adds a richness and the mint adds a new twist on an old Middle-Eastern favorite.

Ingredients:

2 large eggplants - cut in half lengthwise
1/2 cup soft tofu - drained
2-3 Tbsp. lemon juice
1/4 tsp. sea salt
2 cloves garlic - minced
1-2 Tbsp. fresh chopped mint
Fresh ground black pepper to taste

Preparation:

Place eggplants on a lightly oiled baking pan face down and bake at 425° for about 30 minutes until soft. Cool slightly, remove the skins and discard them, and put the eggplant in a food processor. Add the remaining ingredients and blend until smooth. Chill and serve with your favorite crackers, vegetable wedges, or pita breads.

Makes 6 - 8 servings

*"We have no more right
to consume happiness without producing it,
then to consume wealth
without producing it."*

George Bernard Shaw

Tzatziki
Greek Tofu Garlic Dip

Don't worry, it's easier to make than to pronounce. Actually, this has a nice coolness to it; the very thing for a hot afternoon party.

Ingredients:
> 1 lb. soft tofu
> 2-3 garlic cloves
> 1/8 cup fresh mint
> 2 green onions - coarsely chopped
> 1 cup cucumbers - peeled and coarsely chopped
> Juice of one lemon
> 1/4 tsp. of grated lemon rind (zest)
> Sea salt to taste

Preparation:
Place all the ingredients in a food processor and blend until smooth. Serve with your favorite raw veggies, chips, or pretzels. Or heat it and use as a sauce over steamed greens, broccoli, or fresh green beans.

Makes approximately 3 cups

"Whenever you find yourself on the side of the majority, it is time to look back and reflect."

Mark Twain (Samuel Clemmens)

Eggplant Baba Ganoush

Here's a Middle-Eastern favorite. Make it thick and put it on a platter with hummus, tabouli, and tomato wedges. Put it all in pita bread and have a sensory explosion of flavor in your mouth.

Ingredients:

      2 large eggplants
      4-6 Tbsp. lemon juice
      1/4 cup firm tofu - drained
      1/4 cup tahini
      2-3 cloves garlic - minced
      Sea salt and fresh ground black pepper to taste
      2 Tbsp. fresh parsley - chopped
      Cayenne pepper to taste (optional)

Preparation:

Cut the eggplant in half and place it on a lightly oiled baking tray. In a 425° oven, place the eggplant in and bake it until soft, around 30 minutes (or you can steam it until it's soft). Remove from the heat and allow it a few minutes to cool. Scoop out the eggplant from the skins and set aside. In a food processor, combine the eggplant with the rest of the ingredients except the parsley, and blend until smooth. Place it in a bowl, garnish it with the parsley, and chill. Serve with your favorite dipping veggies, or on crackers or fresh pita bread.

Makes 6 - 8 servings

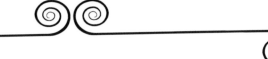

Side Dishes

Portabello Mushrooms in Miso/Basil Sauce

This will drive them wild. Whether meat eater or vegetarian, this is simply divine! Serve this with wild rice and steamed asparagus for the Epicurean delight of your life!

Ingredients:

> 6 Portabello mushrooms - stemmed & sliced
> 2 Tbsp. white or mellow miso
> 1 Tbsp. mirin
> 2 Tbsp. fresh basil - chopped
> 1 large onion - sliced in rings
> 3 cloves garlic - diced
> Water as needed

Preparation:

Combine miso and enough water to dissolve the miso (approximately 3-4 Tbsp.) In a skillet heat the miso and add the onions. Sauté for several minutes, then add the mushrooms. Add more water if needed, cover, and cook for 2 minutes. Add the basil and the mirin, stir well, and recover. Cook 3-5 more minutes, then uncover. Stirring frequently, simmer until almost all of the liquid is reduced. Serve immediately. This sauce can accompany any grain or pasta dish.

Makes 4 - 6 servings

Indian Curried Lentils

This is about the easiest recipe in this book. I've even showed this one to children, which is a good way to get them to eat it. Let them help make it.

Ingredients:

> 2 cups red lentils - rinsed
> 2 cups water
> 2 large onions - chopped
> 2 Tbsp. canola oil
> 1 tsp. each - curry powder, cumin, and chili powder
> 1/2 tsp. turmeric
> Cayenne or fresh ground black pepper to taste

Preparation:

In a large skillet, heat the oil and sauté the onions until soft. Add the spices and sauté for an additional 2 minutes. Add the lentils and the water and bring to a boil. Stir well, reduce the heat, and cover. Cook for approximately 30 minutes, stirring occasionally, or until lentils are tender and all the liquid has been absorbed (you may have to add a little extra water if needed). Goes great with a dollop of tofu sour cream on top (see page 40). Serve with a basmati rice and a steamed green vegetable.

Makes 4 - 6 servings

Stuffed Butternut Squash

Always a seasonal favorite, I can find so many things with which to stuff squash. Here is a good basic recipe to get you started.

Ingredients:

2 butternut squash - washed and halved, with seeds removed
2 cups brown rice - cooked
1 cup walnuts - chopped
1 red bell pepper - chopped
3 stalks celery - chopped
1 large onion - chopped
1 cup firm tofu - mashed
1 tsp. garlic powder
1/2 tsp. each - basil, thyme, and ground sage
2 Tbsp. San-J tamari
2-3 Tbsp. tahini
Cayenne or fresh ground black pepper to taste

Preparation:

Place squashes, face down, on a baking tray. Bake in a 350° oven until tender, but not too soft. Remove from oven and allow to cool. Scoop out the insides into a bowl, being careful not to break the skins, and set the skins aside. In a mixing bowl, combine the remaining ingredients with the squash and mix well. Fill the skins with the mixture and return to the oven for another 20 minutes or until browned.

Makes 4 - 6 servings

Shiitake in Miso

Shiitake is the king of the mushrooms. Their special taste is very distinctive and quite delicious. I highly recommend this fungal treasure. For fresh, locally produced, organic shiitake, see your local markets or consult your local directory for further information. Shiitake are also noted for their antioxidant content, as well as for their flavor. They can also take the place of meat in most recipes, believe it or not...

Ingredients:

20 shiitake (fresh or rehydrated stemmed and cut in half)
3 Tbsp. miso (light or red)
1/2 cup water
2 Tbsp. mirin (sweet cooking wine)
1 tsp. grated ginger
2 Tbsp. rice vinegar
2 green onions - chopped
2 cloves garlic - minced
1 Tbsp. maple syrup/sweetener

Preparation:

Place the 40 shiitake mushroom halves aside. In a blender, combine the remaining ingredients except the onions, adding a little more water if needed. (Should be a thin sauce, but not runny.) Blend to proper consistency and set aside. In a skillet, over medium heat, place the mushrooms and the sauce together and cook, stirring frequently for 2-3 minutes. Reduce the heat, cover, and simmer for another 5 minutes. Add more water if needed. Serve over rice or as a side dish.

Makes 8 - 10 servings

Cajun Red Beans & Dirty Rice

Serve it with fresh salsa and avocado, or a little gumbo.

Ingredients:
>2 cups - cooked red beans
>1 cup tomatoes - diced
>1 cup corn kernels (fresh or frozen)
>1 large onion - chopped
>3 green onions - chopped
>2 carrots - coarsely chopped
>1-2 Jalapeno peppers - seeded and chopped fine
>1 celery stalk - chopped fine
>2 Tbsp. San-J tamari
>1/8 cup fresh cilantro - chopped fine
>1 tsp. ground cumin
>1 Tbsp. chili powder
>1 Tbsp. garlic powder
>2 Tbsp. sesame seeds
>1/2 tsp. fresh ground black pepper (to taste)
>2 cups brown basmati rice
>3 1/2 cups vegetable stock/water
>2 Tbsp. fresh parsley - chopped
>Cayenne pepper to taste

Preparation:
In a pot over a medium heat, add the rice, sesame seeds, and all the dry spices. Stir constantly for 3 minutes or until the rice lightly browns. Add the vegetable stock, tamari, onion, carrots, and celery and bring to a boil. Reduce the heat and simmer for 15 minutes. Add the tomatoes, corn, jalepeno peppers, green onions, and beans and simmer until all the liquid is absorbed. Remove from the heat and toss with cilantro and parsley.

Makes 6 - 8 servings

Mexican Black Bean Combo

The basic rice and bean dish with a little twist. We cook it in the tomato sauce and spices first, so you don't have to try to flavor it afterwards.

Ingredients:

>2 cups black beans (soaked and cooked) or
> 1 can rinsed and drained
>3 cloves garlic - chopped
>1 medium onion - chopped
>1-2 Jalapeno peppers - seeded and diced
>2-3 Roma tomatoes or 1 large tomato - chopped
>1 lemon - juiced
>1 cup tomato juice
>2 cups water
>1 1/2 cup basmati rice (uncooked)
>1/2 cup pumpkin seeds/pepitas - lightly toasted
>2 Tbsp. San-J tamari/soy sauce
>1/8 cup parsley - chopped

Preparation:

In a large covered skillet, over medium heat, add 1 Tbsp. each of tomato juice, water and tamari. Add the garlic and onions and sauté for 2 minutes. Add the peppers, tomatoes, and rice, and sauté 2 more minutes. Add the rest of the tomato juice and the water, stir well, and bring to a boil. Reduce the heat, cover, and simmer until all the water is absorbed (about 20 minutes). Dry and fluff the rice gently with a fork. Mix in the beans, parsley, and pepitas. Sprinkle with the lemon juice and toss.

Makes 6 servings

(Bombay) Indian Tofu & Potato Casserole

The perfect dish that requires a minimum amount of effort. It gives you more time to make the chutney. Serve it with dal, seasoned split peas cooked until soft, and chapatis - a baked flat bread.

Ingredients:

6 cups potatoes (any small kind) don't peel it if possible - sliced
1 1/2 cups green onions - chopped fine
2 Tbsp. fresh ginger - grated
1/2 cup water or vegetable stock
3 Tbsp. San-J tamari
3/4 lb. soft or silken tofu
2 carrots - sliced
1/8 tsp. of the following spices: ground - coriander, turmeric, cumin, cinnamon, cardomon, cayenne, nutmeg and fenugreek (or 1 tsp. curry powder)
1 tsp. each - paprika and parsley for garnish

Preparation:

In a large casserole or baking dish, layer the potatoes. Then cover with the carrots and green onions. In a blender, combine all the remaining ingredients except the paprika and parsley. Blend well, add a little water if needed, and pour over the potato mixture. Sprinkle with the paprika and place in a preheated oven at 425° for 1 hour or until golden brown. Garnish with parsley and serve hot.

Makes 6 - 8 servings

Southern Style
Black Eyed Pea Medley

Whip up a batch of corn bread to go with it. Yeehaw!

Ingredients:
> 2 cups dry black eyed peas (soaked overnight, rinsed well, and drained)
> 1 cup fresh corn kernels
> 1 cup celery - chopped fine
> 1 sweet red bell pepper - chopped fine
> 1 cup carrots - grated
> 2 cups chopped greens (i.e. collards, spinach, etc.)
> 1 large onion - chopped
> 1/2 cup white or rice vinegar
> 1/2 cup cilantro - coarsely chopped
> 1 Tbsp. San-J tamari
> 3 Tbsp. nutritional yeast/Red Star
> Sea salt and pepper to taste

Preparation:
In a large pot, put in peas and just enough water to cover them. Bring to a boil and simmer for 25 minutes. Add the onions and carrots and cook for 2 minutes. Add the corn, pepper, and celery, and cook one more minute. Make sure the peas are tender, then drain, reserving the stock for a later recipe. Cover and set aside. In a small mixing bowl, whisk the vinegar, tamari, and yeast together. Pour over the pea mixture, and sprinkle with cilantro, and toss. Season with salt and pepper to taste. Serve over rice.
Note: This can also be chilled and served on a bed of mixed salad greens and lettuce.

Makes 6 - 8 servings

Vegetables Marseilles

The French never had it this good. Still the same rich flavors, but without most of the fat. The balsamic vinegar and the Dijon mustard blend are the keys to this Napoleonic dream.

Ingredients:

2 cups broccoli - florets and sliced stems
2 cups cauliflower - florets
1 large onion - quartered
1 cup carrots - grated
2 cups mushrooms - sliced
1 large red pepper - cut in large chunks
1 cup whole green olives - pitted

Dressing:

1/4 cup miso (light colored)
1/4 cup water
2 Tbsp. tahini
1/3 cup balsamic vinegar
1 Tbsp. Dijon mustard
2 cloves garlic - minced
1/4 cup fresh parsley
2 tsp. maple syrup/sweetener
1 Tbsp. fresh basil - chopped
1/2 tsp. each - oregano and tarragon
Fresh ground black pepper to taste

Preparation:

In a large pot, steam the cauliflower for 3-5 minutes. Add the onion and steam for 2 more minutes. Add the broccoli and continue to steam until the broccoli is tender, but still crisp. Remove and rinse with cold water. Toss together with the mushrooms, carrots and red pepper, and set aside. In a blender, place all the dressing ingredients and blend until smooth. Place everything except the olives into a shallow dish and allow to marinate for several hours in the refrigerator (the longer the better). Toss thoroughly and garnish with the olives. Serve as is or on a fresh bed of torn lettuce.

Makes 8 servings

"If we could give every individual
the right amount of nourishment and exercise,
not too little and not too much,
we would have found the safest way to health."

Hippocrates

Tofu Caraway Cabbage

The caraway brings a whole new taste to this European favorite. Cooked in a creamy sauce, I'm sure you're going to love it. Serve this with a nice goulash or millet loaf and a salad.

Ingredients:
>1 Tbsp. olive oil
>1 large head of cabbage - sliced in long strips
>1 large onion - chopped
>3 cloves garlic - diced
>1/2 lb. soft tofu
>2 Tbsp. lemon juice
>1/4 tsp. sea salt
>2 Tbsp. each - caraway seeds, water, San-J tamari, and cider vinegar
>1/4 cup fresh parsley
>Fresh ground black pepper to taste

Preparation:
In a skillet, heat the caraway seeds until they start to pop. Add the oil and garlic and sauté. Add the onions and cook until soft. Add the water, tamari, and the vinegar, and stir well. Add the cabbage, cover, and simmer for 10-15 minutes or until the cabbage is tender (add more water if needed). In a blender, combine the tofu, lemon, and salt, and blend until it's smooth. Pour over the cabbage and heat for 1 more minute. Season with fresh pepper and garnish with the parsley.

Makes 6 - 8 servings

Sun Dried Tomatoes
& Basmati Rice

Ingredients:
>2 cups brown basmati rice
>3 3/4 cups water
>1/4 cup San-J tamari
>1 cup sun dried tomatoes - cut in thirds and rinsed
>4 cloves garlic - diced
>3 Tbsp. nutritional yeast/Red Star
>1 Tbsp. olive oil
>1 tsp. cider vinegar
>1/4 tsp. each - oregano, basil, and thyme
>Dash of cayenne pepper

Preparation:
In a large saucepan, heat the water, tamari, and garlic until boiling. Add the rice and reduce heat to a simmer. Add the sun dried tomatoes and continue to simmer (approximately 50-60 minutes) until all the liquid has been absorbed. Uncover, cool, and fluff with a fork. Place in a large mixing bowl. In a small bowl, whisk together the remaining ingredients and toss in with the rice mix. Goes great with fresh broccoli or steamed greens.

Hint: Figure out how long you would steam your favorite veggies and place them on top, accordingly, during the rice cooking. For example: broccoli should be placed on top between 5-7 minutes before the completion of the rice, carrots 10-12 minutes, and they will all finish together using only the one pan.

Makes 4 - 6 servings

Cous Cous with Garden Greens

This is a simple yet delicious meal that's both easy and quick to make. Great for when you don't have a lot of time to spend in the kitchen. Also works well if you have a garden and are growing your own greens. Easy cleanup too!

Ingredients:

> 2 cups whole wheat cous cous
> 4 cups water
> 3-4 Tbsp. San-J tamari
> 3 cloves garlic - diced
> 1 large onion - chopped
> 2 cups steamed greens (i.e., spinach, chard, kale, bok choy, etc.)
> 1/4 cup nutritional yeast/Red Star
> 1/4 tsp. cayenne pepper
> 2 cups sunflower, buckwheat, or other sprouts

Preparation:

In a saucepan, combine the water, tamari, garlic, onions, and cayenne, and bring to a boil. Add the cous cous and remove from heat. Stir in the greens, cover, and let it sit for 5-7 or more minutes. Place the sprouts in a bowl and spoon on the cous cous mixture. Sprinkle with nutritional yeast and lightly toss everything together. Serve with baked tofu chunks for a delicious meal.

Makes 4 servings

Italian Garbanzos & Noodles

What a wonderful dish. Plenty of protein and energy and yet low in fat. If that's not good enough, it's all made in one pan for easy cleanup. What a treat!

Ingredients:

> 2 cups garbanzo beans (soaked, cooked, and drained)
> 2 cups spiral pasta (uncooked)
> 3 cloves garlic - minced
> 1 cup celery - diced
> 1 red bell pepper - seeded and chopped
> 2 carrots - diced
> 1 large onion - chopped
> 2 large tomatoes - chopped with juice
> 1 tsp. each - oregano, basil, and thyme
> Sea salt and fresh ground black pepper to taste
> 3 cups water
> 1 Tbsp. olive oil

Preparation:

In a large skillet or saucepan, heat the oil and sauté the onions and garlic for 2-3 minutes, until the onions start to turn clear. Add the red pepper and sauté another 2 minutes. Add all the other ingredients except the noodles, and bring to a boil. Reduce heat and simmer for 20-25 minutes. Add the noodles and continue to cook, stirring frequently, until the noodles are al dente (firm), about 8-10 minutes, and the stock is reduced down and somewhat thicker. Serve while hot with fresh garlic bread. ***Note:*** You can add some cornstarch dissolved in cool water to the stock to make it thicker.

Makes 6 servings

Bean & Squash Delight

Just the thing for those cool autumn nights. Have this when the squash are in season and plentiful. Guaranteed to fill up even the biggest appetites and yet still be low in fat.

Ingredients:

2 cups haricot beans/white beans (soaked, cooked, and drained)
4 cups butternut or buttercup squash - peeled and cubed
1 large onion - sliced
2 cups mushrooms - sliced
1 green bell pepper - seeded and chopped
1 red bell pepper - seeded and chopped
3 cloves garlic - minced
2 large tomatoes - chopped with juice
1/4 cup cilantro - minced
1 tsp. oregano
1 Tbsp. olive oil (or 1 Tbsp. San-J tamari and 2 Tbsp. water for low fat)
1 jalapeno pepper - seeded and diced
Sea salt and fresh ground black pepper to taste
1 cup water

Preparation:

In a skillet, heat the oil (or San-J tamari/water) and sauté the onions, garlic, and peppers, until onions become clear. Add the remaining ingredients and bring to a boil. Reduce the heat, cover, and simmer for 20-25 minutes or until the squash is soft. Adjust the seasonings and serve. Goes great with rice or pilaf.

Makes 6 servings

Green Beans Almondine

A hit at even the most elegant of dinners, I like to serve this one at catered affairs with a nice lasagna as the main course.

Ingredients:
> 2 lbs. fresh or frozen green beans - washed and stemmed or thawed
> 1 cup almonds - slivered
> 1 large onion - sliced in rings
> 1 cup mushrooms - sliced
> 1/2 cup red bell pepper - chopped
> 2 Tbsp. canola oil or almond oil
> 2 Tbsp. San-J tamari
> Cayenne or fresh ground black pepper to taste

Preparation:
Steam the green beans until just tender (around 4-5 minutes if frozen), then rinse in cold water and set aside. In a skillet, heat the oil and sauté the onion until soft. Add the almonds and mushrooms and cook for several more minutes. Add the red pepper and tamari and cook another minute, then add the beans, stir well, and cook for another 2 minutes. Season with pepper and serve. Makes a great side dish.

Makes 4 - 6 servings

Broccoli & Mushrooms
in Garlic Glaze

*I make this all the time. One of my favorite ways to eat broccoli.
In the time that it takes to cook my rice, this is finished and ready
to eat. What a fabulous dinner!*

Ingredients:

> 1 large head of broccoli - sliced stems and florets
> 2 cups mushrooms - sliced
> 1 large onion - chopped
> 4 cloves garlic - minced
> 1/2 cup red bell pepper - chopped
> 2 Tbsp. San-J tamari
> 1 cup water
> 1 Tbsp. arrowroot powder
> 1 Tbsp. olive oil

Preparation:

In a large skillet, heat the oil and sauté the onions until
soft. Add the garlic, mushrooms, and red pepper, and cook
several more minutes. Add the broccoli and a couple Tbsp.
of water, and cover. Steam for 4-5 minutes or until the
broccoli is tender, but not mushy. In a separate small bowl,
mix the arrowroot, tamari, and the remaining water
together, and pour over the broccoli combo. Stir constantly
over medium heat until the glaze thickens. Remove from
heat and serve with a rice or grain main dish.

Makes 4 - 6 servings

Main Courses

My Sister's Tofu Rainbow Paté

Ingredients:

3 x
- 1 lb. cake of firm tofu
- 2 Tbsp. canola oil
- 1/2 tsp. garlic powder
- 1/2 tsp. onion powder
- 4 Tbsp. nutritional yeast/Red Star
- 3 Tbsp. San-J tamari
- 1 tsp. arrowroot powder
- 1 tsp. powdered vegetable broth or "Spike"
- 1 cup cooked carrots or beets
- 1 cup cooked spinach or broccoli (lightly steamed)
- 1 large onion - chopped

Preparation:

In a food processor, blend the first 8 ingredients with the onion, until creamy smooth. Pour into well-oiled 8" x 3" bread loaf pan. Smooth until level. Repeat same recipe again without the onion, and add the cup of carrots/beets, and blend until creamy smooth. Pour into the same loaf pan on top of the other layer. Do not mix together, just gently smooth until level. Repeat the recipe again, but add the spinach/broccoli instead of the carrots, and 1 tsp. extra of arrowroot (spinach adds extra moisture). Blend again until creamy smooth. Pour into the loaf pan and smooth until level. Bake for 45 minutes at 350°. Allow to cool and place in the refrigerator. Refrigerate for several hours until completely cooled, or overnight. Loosen the edges with flat knife or spatula. Turn the loaf pan over onto a plate and gently tap. The paté should fall out of the loaf pan and hold the shape of the loaf. Slice and serve on a bed of lettuce. Serve for lunch, dinner, or at your next party.

Makes 8 - 10 servings

Tofu Vegetable Loaf

Ingredients:

> 2 lbs. firm tofu - mashed
> 1 Tbsp. olive oil
> 2 slices of whole wheat bread - diced into large pieces
> 1 onion - diced
> 1 green bell pepper - diced
> 1 stalk celery - diced
> 1/2 carrot - diced
> 1 clove garlic - diced
> 1/4 tsp. each - oregano and basil
> Dash dry mustard
> Dash cayenne pepper
> 1/4 cup nutritional yeast/Red Star
> 2 Tbsp. San-J tamari
> 2 Tbsp. tahini (optional)
> 1/4 cup bran, wheat germ, or rolled oats (optional)

Preparation:

Toast the diced bread until lightly browned and add to the mashed tofu. In an oiled skillet, sauté the vegetables until tender. Add the seasonings while sautéing, mix well, then add to the tofu mixture. Place everything in a well-oiled casserole dish. Bake for 40 minutes at 350°. Loosen the edges with a flat knife or spatula. Cool slightly and flip over onto a platter. It should easily come out of the casserole dish. Serve sliced with gravy on top.

Makes 8 - 10 servings

Tofu Manhattan

I got this recipe while staying with friends in Maui. They love to experiment and are very inventive in the kitchen. So I did my best to redo the taste and flavor that came that night as a one time shot, and this is what was born. Thanks for the inspiration!

Ingredients:

> 1 lb. firm tofu cut in 2' strips 1/2" thick
> 1 cup mushrooms - sliced
> 1 medium onion - chopped
> 3-4 large potatoes - washed and chunked
>   (don't peel)
> 2 cups potato water
> 1 tsp. salt
> 1 Tbsp. olive oil
> 2 Tbsp. Braggs Amino Acids or San-J tamari
> 3 cloves garlic - minced
> 2 sprigs rosemary
> 2 Tbsp. arrowroot - dissolved in 1/4 cup water
> 6-8 slices of whole grain bread - toasted
> 1/2 cup soymilk/nut or rice milk
> Cayenne or fresh green black pepper to taste
> Fresh greens for garnish

Preparation:

In 4 cups water, boil the potatoes, onions, and salt. Boil until the potatoes are tender, drain, and reserve the liquid. In a bowl, mash the potatoes and onions with the soy milk. Set aside. In a skillet, heat the oil and brown the tofu. Add the Braggs and rosemary and reduce the heat. Slowly cook the tofu, turning occasionally, until the tofu is chewy.

Add a little potato water, the mushrooms, and garlic, and simmer for two minutes. Add 2 cups of the potato reserve to the tofu, simmer for 5 more minutes, then add the arrowroot and water. Stir until it's thickened, season with pepper, and set aside. To assemble, place a piece of toasted bread on a plate of greens. Cover with mashed potatoes and top with the tofu and sauce.

Makes 6 - 8 servings

"He will be regarded as a benefactor of his race
who shall teach man to confine himself
to a more innocent diet.
Whatever my own practice may be,
I have no doubt that it is part
of the destiny of the human race,
in it's gradual improvement,
to leave off eating animals
as surely as the savage tribes
have left off eating each other."

Count Leo Tolstoy

Brook's Quick Crust Pizza

Ingredients:

Crust:

> 2 cups whole wheat flour
> 1/2 cup gluten flour
> 1 tsp. baking powder (non-aluminum)
> 1/2 tsp. garlic powder
> 1/2 cup water (more or less as needed)
> 2-3 tsp. olive oil
> 1/2 tsp. each - sea salt and baking soda

Tomato sauce: (or your favorite jar pasta sauce)
1 small can of tomato paste
Enough water to thin to desired consistency
1/2 tsp. each - garlic powder, basil, oregano, and thyme
Pinch of sea salt

Veggie toppings: mushrooms, onions, olives, eggplant, zucchini, peppers (red, green & yellow), artichokes, hot peppers of all kinds, broccoli, any other veggies you can think of.

Cheesy topping:
see Moatsarella (page 94)

Preparation:

To prepare the crust, put all the dry ingredients in a bowl and mix together well. Add the water and work together into a ball, then coat with the oil and continue to knead the dough until it's stiff but smooth. Cover and place in a warm place for 20 minutes. Meanwhile, prepare the sauce by adding all the ingredients together and whisking until smooth. Set aside. Prepare your veggie toppings and prepare the cheesy topping per recipe, but don't cook it yet. To assemble, take the dough and roll it out on a board until it's only 1/8" thick. (It will double in size, make it thicker for a thicker crust.) Pinch or bunch up the outer edge to hold the sauce in. Spread the tomato sauce all over the crust up to the edge. Place whatever veggies you decide to use all over the sauce and crust. Cook the cheesy topping until it's thick, as in the recipe, but still liquid and pourable, then cover the pizza with the cheesy topping. Place the pizza in a preheated oven at 450°. Bake approximately 12 minutes or until the crust has turned a deep golden brown. Remove and slice. Serve immediately. (Or stick in the freezer to cool, and eat it cold - one of my favorites. Who can explain?)

Makes 1 medium pizza

"The only way to have a friend
is to be one."

Ralph Waldo Emerson

Tofu Spinach Crepe

Boy, with the amount of protein in this recipe, it's no wonder Popeye was always so strong and full of energy, yet light on his feet. Well, I like spinach too! (Toot, toot!)

Ingredients:

Crepe:
>1/3 cup unbleached flour
>1/2 cup whole wheat pastry flour
>1/4 cup flax seeds
>1 Tbsp. tahini
>1 cup soymilk or nutmilk
>1/8 tsp. sea salt
>Cooking oil to prevent sticking.

>**Note:** Freeze or refrigerate any extra crepes.

Filling:
>2 lbs. firm tofu - drained and mashed
>1/4 cup lemon juice
>1 tsp. sea salt
>1 Tbsp. onion powder
>2 Tbsp. nutritional yeast/Red Star
>1 cup spinach - cooked, drained and chopped
>1 cup pine nuts - roasted
>Fresh ground black pepper to taste

Preparation:

Crepes: In a blender, mix all the ingredients until smooth. Chill for 30 minutes. Heat skillet with a little oil. Over a medium heat, test a few drops of the batter in the skillet to make sure it's heated properly. Pour about 2-3 Tbsp. of batter all at once. Remove the skillet from the heat, tilting the pan in a circular motion, so that the batter spreads to cover most of the bottom of the skillet. Cook until little bubbles appear and edges start to brown. Flip with a spatula and cook the other side until lightly browned. Repeat the process with the remaining batter. Stack the crepes, cover, and set aside.

Filling: In a large mixing bowl, combine all the ingredients thoroughly. Lay out the crepe, spoon 3-4 Tbsp. of filling on it, and roll it up. Lay them seam down in a baking tray, making a single layer. Bake 15-20 minutes at 350°.

Makes approximately 8 - 10 crepes

*"How prompt we are to satisfy
the hunger and thirst of our body;
how slow to satisfy the hunger and thirst
of our souls."*

Henry David Thoreau

Italian Holiday Roll

I saw these at a party one time, stuffed with all kinds of things I don't care to eat, but the idea intrigued me. These are the results of that brainstorming and I think they're quite impressive. Mini lasagnas, so to speak.

Ingredients:

>   12 Lasagna noodles - soaked in warm water until soft
>   1 jar of your favorite pasta sauce
>   2 lbs. firm tofu - drained well
>   1/2 cup nutritional yeast/Red Star
>   1 tsp. each - oregano, basil, thyme
>   1 Tbsp. garlic powder
>   2 green onions - chopped with greens
>   2 Tbsp. fresh parsley - chopped
>   1/4 cup lemon juice
>   1 tsp. sea salt
>   1/2 cup pine nuts

Preparation:

In a bowl, mash the tofu and mix together the yeast, oregano, basil, thyme, garlic, onions, lemon juice, and salt. Combine thoroughly with the tofu to make the filling. Take the soft noodles, lay out flat one at a time, and cover the length with about 3 Tbsp. of filling. Spread evenly, then roll the noodle up from one end to the other. Stand the rolls up on end in a baking dish that already has a thin layer of sauce in it. When all 12 noodles are rolled up, cover with the remaining pasta sauce. Sprinkle the pine nuts and parsley on top and bake, covered, for 20 minutes at 350°. Uncover, bake 5 more minutes, and serve.

Makes 12 rolls

Soy Burgers

Another example of how many ways there are to make a burger!

Ingredients:
>2 1/2 cups soybeans (soaked, cooked, and drained)
>1 cup brown rice - cooked
>1 cup millet - cooked
>1/4 cup rolled oats
>1/4 cup San-J tamari
>1/4 cup water
>1 large onion - chopped fine
>1 Tbsp. each - garlic powder, basil, and parsley
>1 tsp. dry mustard
>Cayenne or fresh ground black pepper to taste

Preparation:
In a food processor, combine the soybeans, tamari, water, oats, and spices together. Place in a large bowl and add the remaining ingredients. Mix well and form into patties. Can be frozen at this point for later use (with wax paper in between each patty), or place on a lightly oiled baking tray and bake in a 375° oven for 10 minutes. Turn and repeat until browned.

Makes about a dozen burgers

"Be kind whenever it is possible;
It is always possible."

Dalai Lama

Simple Soy Burgers

Sounds like a nursery rhyme, and why not? They're easy, incredibly healthy, and kids just eat them up. Make double batches and freeze them for convenience. Hint: Put waxed paper between each burger.

Ingredients:

2 1/2 cups soybeans - cooked
1/2 cup firm tofu
1 medium onion - chopped
1/2 cup water or vegetable stock
1/2 cup whole wheat flour
2 Tbsp. tahini
Sea salt and fresh ground pepper to taste.

Preparation:

Place the soybeans in a food processor and blend for 20 seconds. Add the rest of the ingredients and mix together until the batter balls up and is stiff and thick enough to make patties with. (Add a little more water if it's too dry or more flour if it's too wet.)

Shape into patties and place on a lightly oiled baking tray. Bake at 400° (approximately 15-20 minutes), flipping them half way through, until both sides are browned. Serve on whole grain bun with your favorite toppings and condiments.

Makes 6 burgers

Tofu Pecan Loaf

This recipe is what I think the perfect family holiday meal should be built around. Garnished and served with stuffing, sides, salads, and deserts!

Ingredients:
>1 1/2 lbs. firm tofu - drained
>1 1/2 cups pecans - chopped fine
>1 large onion - chopped
>2 cloves garlic - chopped
>1/8 cup tahini
>2 carrots - grated
>2 Tbsp. arrowroot
>1/4 cup oat flour (or ground oats)
>1/8 cup nutritional yeast/Red Star
>1 tsp. garlic powder
>1/2 tsp. basil
>1/2 tsp. savory (herb)
>Sea salt and ground pepper to taste
>Enough San-J tamari and water (one to one ratio) to sauté with.

Preparation:
In a skillet, sauté the onion in tamari and water for 3 minutes. Add the garlic and sauté 2 more minutes. In a food processor, combine the tofu, yeast, spices, tahini, and arrowroot, and blend well. Add the onion mixture and pulse well. Add the carrots and pulse slightly. Add the oat flour and nuts, and pulse just enough to mix together. Pour into an oiled loaf pan and bake in a preheated oven at 375° for one hour or until the top is nicely browned. Cool for a few minutes before serving with your favorite gravy.

Makes 6 - 8 servings

Mushroom Crepe with Bechamel Sauce

I first had crepes in Montreal, Canada. I ate one and thought they were so light, but after trying to finish my third one I saw how deliciously filling they really are. "Bon appetit!"

Ingredients:

2 Tbsp. canola oil
2 lbs. mushrooms - sliced
4 green onions - sliced reserve some tops for garnish
1 large onion - chopped
4 cloves garlic - minced
1/2 tsp. dry tarragon
1 tsp. dry basil
2 Tbsp. balsamic vinegar
2 tsp. maple syrup
1 lb. firm tofu undrained
1-2 Tbsp. San-J tamari or 1 tsp. sea salt
Crepe recipe from Tofu-Spinach Crepes (page 132)

Bechamel Sauce:

2 Tbsp. olive oil
1/2 cup unbleached flour
1/2 tsp. salt
2 cups soymilk or nutmilk
1 Tbsp. tahini
1/2 tsp. turmeric
Cayenne pepper to taste

Preparation:
In a saucepan, heat 1 Tbsp. of the oil and all the flour, and lightly brown. Add all the remaining sauce ingredients and whisk thoroughly. Continue to stir until the sauce thickens. Do not allow to boil! Set aside. In a skillet, heat the remaining oil and sauté the onions, half the garlic, green onions (except garnish), and the mushrooms, until the onions are soft. Add the tarragon and basil and remove from the heat. In a food processor, combine the tofu, vinegar, tamari, the other half of garlic, and the maple syrup together until creamy. Combine with the sauté. (Reserve a few of the mushrooms in the sauté for a garnish.) Spoon about 3 Tbsp. of the mushroom filling into each crepe. Roll it up and place it seam down in a baking dish, making a single layer. Bake at 425° for 15 minutes or until browned. To serve, pour the Bechamel sauce over the top of each crepe. Garnish it with mushrooms and green onions.

Makes 8 - 10 servings

"As we are, so we do;
and as we do, so is it done to us;
we are the builders of our fortunes."

Ralph Waldo Emerson

Black Bean Tamale Pie

One of my favorite Mexican foods. This one will fill you up pleasantly. So, loosen your belts and dig in!

Ingredients:

- 2 cups corn meal
- 4 1/2 cups-water (purified)
- 2 cups black beans - cooked
- 2 cups corn (fresh or frozen)
- 1 large onion - chopped
- 1-2 Jalapeno or chilies - seeded and chopped
- 1 cup tomato sauce
- Sea salt and fresh ground black pepper to taste
- 1 tsp. chili powder
- Tofu Sour Cream (page 40)
- Chopped parsley for garnish

Preparation:

Combine the corn meal, water, and salt, and mix until a mushy consistency has been obtained. Set aside. In 2 Tbsp. of water, sauté the onions until transparent. Add the remaining ingredients and simmer for 5 minutes. In a baking dish, take half the cornmeal and make a flat layer across the bottom. Add the bean mixture to form a middle layer and cover with the remaining cornmeal to form a third layer. Place in a preheated 425° oven for one hour or until browned. Garnish with Tofu Sour Cream and fresh chopped parsley.

Makes 6 - 8 servings

Marinated Mock Chicken Tofu

This is the kind of recipe that can be added to any kind of vegetable dish to give it a chewy kind of texture, and enrich the flavor and protein content.

Ingredients:

1 lb. firm tofu - drained well
2 Tbsp. San-J tamari
1 tsp. ground sage
1/2 cup - water
2 Tbsp. - nutritional yeast/Red Star
Fresh ground black pepper to taste
1 Tbsp. imitation chicken soup stock (vegetarian)

Preparation:

Drain tofu well, slice into 1/2 inch thickness, and then place in a towel to dry even more. Cube the tofu or cut into strips. Place in a glass casserole dish and place into a 425° preheated oven. Cook until the tofu starts to get golden brown. Mix the tamari, imitation chicken stock, water, sage, and pepper together, and pour over the tofu. Using a spatula, loosen the tofu and coat them completely with the marinade. Sprinkle the yeast over the top, coating each piece, and return to the oven. Cook for 15 minutes, then turn off the oven. Allow the tofu to remain in the oven for another hour without opening the door. Remove and serve. Can be eaten as is, or with a sauce. Add to a stir-fry or other dishes. Makes a great appetizer.

Makes about 36 1-inch cubes

Spicy Tofu & Broccoli with Roasted Pepitas

Getting away from the usual tomato taste, this South of the Border recipe relies on the sesame and the pepitas for a unique and different blend. But the Jalapeno still says, "Olé!"

Ingredients:

1/2 cup pepitas (pumpkin seeds)
3 Tbsp. San-J tamari and with extra to sprinkle on the pepitas
1 lb. firm tofu - cubed
4 cloves garlic - sliced
2 Tbsp. sesame oil
2 Tbsp. water
2 cups broccoli - florets and stems
1 cup mushrooms - sliced
1 medium onion - sliced in rings
1 Jalapeno pepper - chopped
1 cup corn - fresh or frozen
1 1/2 Tbsp. nutritional yeast/Red Star

Preparation:

In a skillet, over medium-high heat, heat the pepitas, shaking or stirring, until they all pop (or most do). Sprinkle with tamari, remove from the heat, stir well, and set aside in a small bowl. In the same skillet, heat half the oil over medium heat and brown the tofu. Turn every few minutes, until they're light brown on all sides. Add the remaining oil and garlic and cook for 2 minutes, stirring frequently. Add the mushrooms and onions and cook for 2 more minutes. Add the broccoli stems and pepper and cook for 2 more minutes. Add the broccoli florets, corn, water, and the tamari. Cover and cook for 3-5 minutes or until the broccoli is tender but still crisp and bright green. Sprinkle on the yeast and toss well. Sprinkle on the pepitas for a garnish and serve with rice or somen noodles.

Makes 4 servings

"The obligations of law and equity
reach only to mankind,
but kindness and beneficence should be extended
to the creatures of every species,
and these will flow from the breast of a true man, as
streams that issue from the living fountain."

Plutarch

Tropical Salsa Over Lentils

What would you expect from a guy on a diet, who loves Mexican food and lives in Hawaii? Well, now you know! Actually it's really good, if you're not strict about food combining.

Ingredients:

> 1 cup brown lentils - rinsed and drained
> 2 mangoes - skinned and seeded
> 1 red bell pepper - chopped
> 1 green bell pepper - chopped
> 1 cup tomatoes - chopped
> 1 Jalapeno pepper - seeded (2 if you like it spicy)
> 4 Tbsp. lemon juice
> 1 Tbsp. fresh mint
> 1 Tbsp. fresh coriander or parsley - chopped fine
> 4 green onions - chopped fine
> 2 bay leaves
> Sea salt and fresh ground pepper to taste
> Tortilla chips for dipping
> 1/2 cup - soft tofu
> 3 cloves fresh garlic - minced

Preparation:

In a pot, cover the lentils, garlic, and bay leaves with water, and bring to a boil. (You can add a pinch of salt.) Reduce the heat and simmer about 35 minutes or until the lentils are tender. Remove from the heat, drain, remove the bay leaves, and set aside. In a blender, combine the mango, jalapeno, 2 Tbsp. lemon juice, mint, and the red pepper together, and blend for 30 seconds. In a bowl, combine the green pepper, tomatoes, green onions, and the mango blend, and toss together. Season with salt and pepper and set aside. To make the tofu sour cream, place the tofu and the remaining lemon juice in a blender and blend until smooth, adding salt to taste. To assemble everything, arrange some greens on a platter and spoon the lentils in the center area. Surround the lentils with the chips. Pour the salsa over the lentils and top with the tofu sour cream. Garnish with the fresh coriander or parsley.

Makes 6 - 8 servings

"Nothing is more powerful than an individual
acting out of his conscience,
thus helping to bring
the collective conscience to life."

Norman Cousins

Tofu Mexican Wraps

This is a quick lunch or snack food that appeals to everyone. Personally, I love to load this with hot peppers as well. For a nice change, sauté some onions and peppers and mix them in.

Ingredients:

>   1 lb. firm tofu
>   1/8 cup nutritional yeast/Red Star
>   3-4 Tbsp. San-J tamari
>   2 Tbsp. tahini
>   1 Tbsp. chili powder
>   Cayenne to taste
>   1 tsp. garlic powder
>   1 medium sweet onion - diced
>   1 large tomato - diced
>   2 carrots - grated
>   6 whole wheat tortillas wrappers
>   Enough lettuce for 6 wraps - wash, dried
>   and veined
>   Enough sprouts for 6 wraps (buckwheat or clover)

Preparation:

In a bowl, mash the tofu, add all the spices, and mix together well. Add the tomatoes and onions, and mix thoroughly. Lay out 1 tortilla wrap. Spoon 3 Tbsp. on one end of the wrap. Cover with grated carrot, lettuce, and sprouts, and tuck and roll the wrapper into a cylinder. Repeat until all the wrappers are used. Makes a great lunch or snack. Use the tofu filling as a snack dip as well.

Makes 6 wraps

Roasted Eggplant with Tofu Garlic Sauce

Rubbing the eggplant with the lemon and salt will keep it from oxidizing and discoloring.

Ingredients:

> 2 medium eggplants - peeled and sliced
> 1 lemon
> 1 whole garlic (about 12-14 cloves)
> 1/2 lb. soft tofu
> 3 Tbsp. fresh dill
> 3 Tbsp. cilantro or Italian parsley
> 1/2 cup walnuts
> 1/2 cup celery - chopped
> Sea salt and fresh ground black pepper

Preparation:

Preheat the oven to 425°. Juice the lemon. Take the squeezed lemon and rub the eggplant slices with it. Grate 1/2 tsp. of the lemon peel (zest) and set it aside. Rub the eggplant with salt and place it in a baking dish. Place the peeled garlic on top of the eggplant. Put it in the oven, turning it occasionally, until the eggplant is browned (about 20 minutes). Then, in a food processor, add the tofu, dill, lemon juice, parsley, and 1/2 the roasted garlic, and puree until smooth. Add the walnuts and celery, and lightly pulse them in, keeping it a little chunky. Season with salt and pepper to taste. Pour the blended mixture over the roasted eggplant and remaining garlic. Return it to the oven for another 15-20 minutes or until the tofu edges start to brown. Serve hot over fettuccine noodles.

Makes 6 - 8 servings

Vietnamese Tofu and Noodles

This delicious dish reminds me a lot of Pad Thai noodles.

Ingredients:

    1 lb. firm tofu - rinsed, drained, and cubed
    1/8 cup San-J tamari
    1/8 cup water
    2 Tbsp. fresh grated ginger
    2 Tbsp. garlic - minced
    1 lb. rice noodles
    2 Tbsp. palm sugar/or unrefined sweetener
    1 tsp. crushed red pepper (or to taste)
    1 large onion - chopped
    1 cup snow peas in pods
    4 green onions - chopped
    1/2 cups mushrooms - sliced
    1 cup mung bean sprouts
    Chopped parsley garnish

Preparation:

Mix the tamari, water, ginger, garlic, and red pepper together, and pour over the cubed tofu. Marinate it for at least 30 minutes (the longer the better). Turn the cubes in the marinade at least once. Pour enough boiling water over the noodles to cover them and set aside.
Drain the tofu and reserve the marinade. In a skillet, add 1/2 the marinade and sauté the onions for 3 minutes. Add the tofu and mushrooms, and cook until the liquid is almost gone. Mix sweetener with the remaining marinade, add it and the noodles to the skillet, and toss well. Add the peas and sprouts, and continuously toss for 1-2 minutes until the peas are bright green and the sprouts are slightly wilted.

Makes 6 - 8 servings

Tofu (Chicken) in Artichoke Sauce

My friend loves artichokes so much, I had to invent this sauce for him. Poured over the tofu chicken, it makes a whole new kind of flavor. So thanks a lot for the idea, Breeze.

Ingredients:

1 lb. firm tofu - cut in 1/4 inch thick x 2 inch pieces
2 Tbsp. imitation chicken stock
1 cup water
1 Tbsp. olive oil
1 medium onion - sliced
2 cloves garlic - minced
2 medium tomatoes - seeded and chopped
1 cup artichoke hearts
1 Tbsp. fresh basil - chopped fine
1/4 cup fresh parsley - chopped
1 Tbsp. nutritional yeast flakes/Red Star
Sea salt and fresh ground black pepper to taste

Preparation:

In a baking pan, arrange the tofu in a single layer. Mix the chicken stock with the water and set aside. Bake the tofu at 425° for 20 minutes. Turn and repeat. Remove from the oven and add the stock. Allow to marinate for 30 minutes, turning at least once. Heat the oil and sauté the onions and garlic until the onions become soft. When ready, drain the tofu and pour the marinade and remaining ingredients except the tomatoes and tofu, in a blender, and blend until smooth. Toss the tofu and tomatoes together, cover with the sauce, and return to the oven for another 15 minutes or until browned.

Makes 4 - 6 servings

Mexican Black Beans

As you can see, I like Mexican and Southwest cooking. It's important that the tastes are authentic, and what more basic dish is there than black beans? You'll find them "bueno!"

Ingredients:

8 oz. (1/2 lb.) black beans - soaked overnight, drained, and rinsed well
2 large onions - chopped
1/2 lb. mushrooms - sliced
1 red pepper - coarsely chopped
1 green pepper
6 garlic cloves - chopped
1 28 oz. can - crushed tomatoes
1 small can tomato paste
2 Tbsp. chili powder
1 tsp. cumin
2 Tbsp. coriander - chopped
Sea salt to taste
Fresh ground black pepper to taste
Cayenne pepper or tabasco sauce to taste
2 bay leaves
Parsley - garnish chopped
Tofu sour cream enough for 6 bowls (page 40)

Preparation:

Place the beans, bay leaves, 2 crushed garlic cloves, and 1/3 the onions in a pot. Cover with water and bring to a boil. Reduce heat and simmer for 1 hour or until beans are tender. Drain, reserving some of the stock. Remove bay leaves. In a skillet, add some of the stock and sauté the remaining onions and garlic until the onions turn clear. Add the peppers and a little more stock and cook several more minutes. Add the mushrooms, tomatoes, paste, and all the spices except the parsley. Use a little more stock if necessary. Finally, add the beans, cover, and simmer for about 30 minutes, checking the liquid often. Cook until most of the liquid is reduced and the bean sauce is fairly thick. Spoon into the bowls and place a dollop of tofu sour cream on top of each one and garnish them with fresh chopped parsley. Serve with tortilla chips or fresh baked corn bread.

Makes 6 servings

*"When I am working on a problem
I never think about beauty.
I only think about how to solve the problem.
But when I have finished,
if the solution is not beautiful,
I know it is wrong."*

Buckminster Fuller

Mexican Tofu Medley

Quite a south of the border meal. Just add some salad and rice and you've got a dinner fit for a "caballero" - Olé!

Ingredients:
> 1 lb. firm tofu - rinsed, drained, and cubed
> 1 Tbsp. tomato paste
> 3 garlic cloves - crushed
> 2 onions - chopped
> 2 cups corn - (fresh or frozen)
> 1 red pepper - chopped
> 1 green pepper - chopped
> 1 1/2 cups zucchini - cut in 1/4 inch slices
> 1 1/2 cups yellow squash - cut in 1/4 inch slices
> 1 Tbsp. arrowroot or cornstarch
> 1/4 cup fresh cilantro - chopped

Marinade:
> 1 cup water
> 3 Tbsp. San-J tamari
> 1 tsp. cumin
> 2 Tbsp. chili powder - mild
> 1 jalapeno pepper - chopped fine

Preparation:
In a baking dish, marinate the tofu in the water, tamari, cumin, chili powder, and jalapeno, for at least 30 minutes (turning at least once). Preheat the oven, drain the tofu, and reserve the marinade. Place the marinated tofu in a 350° oven for 35-40 minutes or until dry and chewy. In a skillet, on a medium heat, pour in 1/2 the marinade and

the garlic, and cook 2 for minutes. Stir in the tomato paste and the tomatoes. Add the onions, peppers, zucchini, and squash. Cover, and cook for 5 more minutes. Add the peas and corn, and cook 3-5 more minutes. Add the arrowroot to the remaining marinade, mix well, and add to the skillet, stirring constantly until it thickens. Mix in the cilantro and tofu and toss thoroughly. Serve with rice or polenta..

Makes 6 - 8 servings

"Cowardice asks the question, "Is it safe?"
Expediency asks the question, "Is it polite?"
Vanity asks the question,
"Is it popular?"
But conscience asks the question,
"Is it right?"
And there comes a point
when one must take a position
that is neither safe, polite, nor popular,
but he must take it because
his conscience tells him that it is right."

Dr. Martin Luther King Jr.

Tofu & Peas in Red Cream

A very European-type dish. I like to serve this one with a good black or pumpernickel bread to soak up the juice.

Ingredients:

>   1 lb. firm tofu - drained and cubed
>   4 cups fresh/frozen peas - thawed and drained
>   3-4 stalks of celery - chopped
>   2 large sweet or red onions - chopped
>   2 Tbsp. olive oil
>   1/4 cup whole wheat flour
>   3/4 cup each - water and tomato juice
>   3-4 Tbsp. San-J tamari
>   1/4 cup chives or green onions - chopped

Preparation:

Place the tofu in a baking dish. In a preheated 425° oven, place the tofu in the oven and bake for 30 minutes. Turn and continue cooking the tofu until it's semi-dry and a little chewy. Heat half the oil in a skillet and sauté the onions until tender. Add the remaining oil and flour, and stir constantly for 20-30 seconds. Still stirring, add the water, juice and tamari, and simmer for several minutes. Add the tofu and simmer for 10 more minutes. Add the celery and peas, stir well, and cover. Cook for 5-10 more minutes. Pour into a serving bowl and garnish with the chives.

Makes 4 - 6 servings

Tofu Yung

This eggless version of the well-known Chinese omelet can fool even the best critics. The key to a firm patty is the use of tahini as the binder, and draining the tofu as thoroughly as possible.

Ingredients:

1 lb. firm tofu - mashed
1 Tbsp. tahini
2 Tbsp. San-J tamari
2 cloves garlic - minced
1 medium carrot - shredded
2 cups mung bean sprouts
Fresh ground pepper to taste
1 tsp. turmeric

Sauce:

4 Tbsp. mirin or 3 Tbsp. maple syrup
3 Tbsp. rice vinegar
2 Tbsp. San-J tamari
1 1/2 cups water
1 1/2 Tbsp. arrowroot/cornstarch

Preparation:

Sauce: Combine all the ingredients in a medium sauce pan and heat over a medium heat, stirring frequently until the sauce thickens. Remove from the heat and set aside. In a mixing bowl, combine all the remaining ingredients. Mix well and press into small patties. Place on a lightly oiled baking tray and place in a preheated 375° oven for 15-20 minutes or until browned. Remove and top with some of the sauce. Serve with rice and steamed broccoli.

Makes 4 servings

Potato Curry with Scalloped Bananas

A true curry, this one gets it's character from the bananas. A great looking dish to serve your guests, and one they will remember.

Ingredients:
Curry:
> 1 Tbsp. canola oil
> 3 cloves garlic - chopped fine
> 1 medium onion - chopped
> 4 cups potatoes (washed, cubed, and steamed)
> 2 carrots - sliced
> 3 cups coconut milk
> 3 Tbsp. cornstarch
> 1 Tbsp. each - curry powder, maple syrup,
> and fresh grated ginger
> 2 Tbsp. San-J tamari
> Cooked basmati rice for 4 people

Bananas:
> 6 bananas - firm
> 1/4 cup soy milk (or nut milk)
> 3/4 cup corn flakes (crushed)
> 2 Tbsp. canola oil
> 1 1/2 Tbsp. tahini
> 1/2 tsp. sea salt
> Ground nutmeg for garnish

Preparation:
In a skillet, heat 1 Tbsp. of oil and sauté the onions and garlic until soft. Add the carrots, curry, ginger, tamari, and maple syrup, and mix well. Add the cornstarch to the coconut milk and stir until it's dissolved. Add to the sauté and stir until the sauce thickens. Reduce heat, and add the potatoes. Cover, and simmer for about 10-15 minutes. Add more water if needed. In another skillet, heat the remaining oil. Slice the bananas into strips 2-3 inches long. Combine the soymilk, tahini, and salt. Whisk until the mixture thickens enough to coat and dip the bananas in, covering them well. Roll the bananas in the corn flakes and place them in the skillet. (You could also bake them in the oven to reduce the amount of fat used.) Cook until they're lightly browned, turn, and repeat. To serve, mound the rice onto a platter and indent the center. Pour the curry into the center and surround the outer rim with the bananas. Sprinkle everything with nutmeg, and serve.

Makes 4 - 6 servings

"The sun, with all those planets revolving around it
and dependent on it,
can still ripen a bunch of grapes
as if it had nothing else in the universe to do."

Galileo

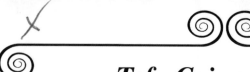

Tofu Cajun Gumbo

A touch of the bayou, and yet with the sea vegetables, you can still have that fish taste without having to use shrimp or fish parts. Spice it like you care to and enjoy. "Ooowee good!"

Ingredients:

1 lb. firm tofu - rinsed, pressed, and drained
2 cups onions - chopped
1 1/2 cups tomatoes - crushed or processed
2 cups water or vegetable stock
2 carrots - sliced
3 celery stalks - chopped
1 cup corn (fresh or frozen)
3 cups okra - stemmed and sliced
1 cup yellow squash - cubed
1 green bell pepper - chopped
1 red pepper - chopped
6 garlic cloves - crushed
1 Tbsp. paprika
1/2 tsp. each - fennel, coriander, and fenugreek
1 tsp. cumin
Cayenne, sea salt, and fresh ground black pepper
   to taste
1/8 cup - arame, kelp, dulse, or other sea
   vegetable, dried and chopped

Preparation:

Cube the tofu into 1 inch pieces. Preheat the oven to 350°. On a baking tray, place the tofu and bake for 40 minutes, turning the tofu at least once, until the tofu is dried and a little chewy. Meanwhile, in a large pot, combine everything

except the tofu, okra, green pepper, salt, and pepper.
Bring to a boil, reduce heat, and simmer for 15 minutes.
Add the okra, green pepper, and salt and pepper, and
simmer for 15 more minutes. Add the tofu and simmer 5
more minutes. Take off the heat, but keep covered for 5-10
more minutes, to allow the flavors to marry. Serve over
rice, with fresh baked cornbread. Deeeeelicious !!!

Makes 8 - 10 servings

"When you cannot get a compliment
in any other way,
pay yourself one."

Mark Twain

Tofu Nut Bake

The simple addition of the nuts allows the tofu to take on a whole new flavor. This is a very grounding dish that's guaranteed to take care of even the most hearty appetites.

Ingredients:
> 1 lb. soft tofu - mashed
> 3 onions sliced in rings
> 2 carrots - grated
> 2 Tbsp. San-J tamari
> 1/2 cup vegetable juice
> 1/2 cup walnuts - ground
> 1/2 cup hazelnuts or Brazil nuts - ground
> 1 clove garlic - crushed or minced

Preparation:
Using a small amount of the vegetable juice, sauté the onions and garlic until the onions are clear. Combine the sauté with the rest of the ingredients in a large mixing bowl. Put the mixture in a baking pan and shape as desired. Place in a preheated oven on 350° for 50-60 minutes. Serve with your choice of gravy and steamed vegetables.

Makes 4 - 6 servings

"When one tugs at a single thing in nature, he finds it attached to the rest of the world."

John Muir

Curried Millet & Tofu

Ingredients:

      1 lb. firm tofu well drained
      3/4 cup millet
      1 small onion - chopped
      1 Tbsp. olive oil
      2 cloves garlic - minced
      1-2 tsp. curry powder (to taste)
      1 tsp. fresh grated ginger
      11/2 cups water
      1 tsp. nutritional yeast/Red Star
      Sea salt and fresh ground black pepper to taste

Preparation:

In a skillet, roast the millet until the aroma comes through and set aside. Heat the oil and sauté the onions and the garlic for several minutes. Add the ginger and tofu and cook several more minutes. Add the curry and yeast and cook 2 more minutes, until the tofu is well coated. Add the millet and water, and bring to a boil. Reduce the heat to a simmer and season with salt and pepper. Cover, and allow to cook for about 30 minutes, or until all the water has been reduced. Remove from the heat and allow to sit undisturbed for another 5-10 minutes. Toss well and serve.

Makes 4 - 6 servings

"I find that the harder I work, the more luck I have."

Thomas Jefferson

Shiitake & Tofu
with Peanut Sauce

This oriental delight uses shiitake and breaded tofu, baked, to give this a true chewy texture. Topped with the creamy rich sweet and sour peanut sauce, it's sure to be a big hit in your family or circle.

Ingredients:

1 lb. firm tofu - cut into 1 inch cubes
1 cup shiitake mushrooms - stemmed and sliced
1 Tbsp. canola oil
2 green onions - chopped
1 cup mung bean sprouts
2 Tbsp. each - tahini, San-J tamari, and water
1/4 cup each - whole wheat flour and
nutritional yeast/Red Star

Sauce:

1/4 cup peanut butter - chunky
2 Tbsp. rice vinegar
1 Tbsp. raw or coconut sugar (use more if you
prefer a sweeter sauce)
1 medium onion - chopped
2-3 Tbsp. San-J tamari
1/2 cup water
1/2 tsp. dried crushed red pepper

Preparation:

In a shallow baking dish, arrange the tofu in a single layer and bake in a 350° oven for 30 minutes. Turn and repeat. Bake until the tofu is chewy, but not crisp.

Allow it to cool for a moment. Meanwhile, in a small bowl, mix the tahini, tamari, and water together, and pour over the tofu. Coat all the tofu thoroughly. Next, combine the flour and yeast together, and sprinkle over the tofu, rolling the squares around in it, until everything is well coated. Return to the oven, place on top rack, DO NOT TURN, and bake for approximately 20 minutes or until browned. Meanwhile, make the sauce. In a skillet, take 2 Tbsp. each of tamari and water, heat, and sauté the onion until soft. Reduce the heat and add the peanut butter and remaining sauce ingredients. Stir until smooth and set aside. In a skillet, heat the oil and sauté the mushrooms and sprouts for several minutes, until the sprouts start to wilt. To serve, place the tofu on a platter, cover with the mushrooms and sprouts, and pour the sauce over the top. Garnish with green onions and serve with your favorite rice or noodles.

Makes 4 servings

"Nowhere can man find a quieter
or untroubled retreat
than in his own soul."

Marcus Aurelius

Lentil & Bulghur with Tofu Cutlets

Ingredients:

1 lb. firm tofu - cut into 1/4 inch thick slices
1/4 cup San-J tamari
1 Tbsp. nutritional yeast/Red Star
1 tsp. garlic powder
1/4 cup water
1/2 cup brown lentils - soaked overnight, cooked
   and drained (about 30 minutes)
1 large onion - chopped
1 red bell or sweet pepper - chopped
1 hot pepper - seeded and diced
1 Tbsp. canola oil
3 cloves garlic - diced
1 cup bulghur wheat
4 Tbsp. lemon juice
1 1/2 cups water (hot)
2 Tbsp. tahini
1/2 tsp. allspice
1/2 tsp. cumin
1/2 cup chopped parsley
Sea salt and fresh ground black pepper to taste

Preparation:

In a preheated 400° oven, place the tofu cutlets in a shallow baking dish and place on the top rack. Turn in 20 minutes and repeat. Prepare a marinade with the tamari, 1/4 of water, nutritional yeast, and garlic. Pour over the cutlets and allow them to soak for 5 minutes on each side. Place them back in the oven until the liquid is mostly gone. Turn off the heat, but leave them in the oven. In a skillet, heat the oil and sauté the garlic for 2 minutes. Add the bulghur and cook for 1 minute more. Add the hot water and the rest of the ingredients except the parsley, and cook covered for about 5-7 minutes or until the bulghur is tender. Add water if needed. Serve the bulghur on a platter with the cutlets arranged on top. Garnish with parsley and serve.

Makes 6 - 8 servings

*"We should not let our fears hold us back
from pursuing our hopes."*

John F. Kennedy

Vietnamese Stir Fry

If chefs were diplomats there'd be no wars. We'd just sit everyone down, and make them eat until they surrendered of their own free will. So enjoy this wondrous gift of peaceful food.

Ingredients:

> 1 lb. firm tofu - drained well and cubed
> 1 Tbsp. canola oil
> 1/2 cup green onions - chopped
> 2 carrots - sliced Julienne style
> 2 cups broccoli florets
> 1 cup broccoli stems - sliced thin
> 2 cups mung bean sprouts
> 1/2 lb. sliced mushrooms
> 1/2 cup each hot peppers, bamboo shoots and
>   water chestnuts - all optional

Marinade:

> 4 cloves garlic - minced
> 1/4 cup San-J tamari
> 1/4 cup water
> 1 Tbsp. ginger - fresh grated
> 1 Tbsp. rice vinegar
> 2 Tbsp. Mirin/or 1 Tbsp. maple syrup

Preparation:
In a shallow dish, place the tofu in a single layer. In a mixing bowl, combine the marinade ingredients together. Mix well and pour over the tofu. Allow it to marinate for at least 30 minutes (the longer the better), turning at least once. In a wok or skillet, heat the oil and cook the carrots for 2 minutes. Next add the broccoli stems and cook for 1 minute. Add the florets, cook 1 more minute, and set aside. Drain the tofu, reserving the marinade. Add the tofu to the wok with a Tbsp. of the marinade. Cook, stirring frequently, until browned. Add the onions and mushrooms and cook for 1 more minute. Add all the other ingredients and the remaining marinade. Cover for 2-3 minutes until the veggies are tender and serve with your favorite rice.

Makes 6 - 8 servings

"Argue for your limitations and sure enough, they're yours."

Richard Bach

Hot & Sour Tofu & Noodles

Ingredients:

> 1 12 oz. package of rice noodles (any width)
> 1/8 cup mirin/unrefined sweetener (maple or rice
>   syrups are nice)
> 1/4 cup rice vinegar
> 3 Tbsp. San-J tamari
> 3 Tbsp. water
> 1/2 lb. firm tofu - rinsed and drained
> 1 tsp. curry powder
> 1 tsp. ginger fresh grated
> Cayenne to taste
> 1 cup cabbage - sliced thin - Julienne
> 1 red onion - sliced thin
> 1 Tbsp. nutritional yeast/Red Star

Preparation:

Place rice noodles in a bowl and cover with boiling water.
Mix the sweetener, vinegar, tamari, water, and ginger, and
marinate the tofu for at least 30 minutes, turning once or
twice. (Can be left overnight in the refrigerator for a more
robust flavor.) When it's ready, remove the tofu, but
reserve the marinade, and place the tofu in a skillet, on
a low heat, turning it frequently. When it's browned, add
a little of the marinade, the curry powder, and onions.
Sauté for 2 minutes, add the yeast and cayenne, and
mix well. Drain and add the noodles and the rest of the
marinade. Mix well and sauté for 1 more minute. Add the
cabbage and cook until it's just getting soft. Remove
and serve.

Makes 4 - 6 servings

Tofu Indian Delight with Mango Chutney

Just like most Indian dishes, this one is fun to eat with chapatis (a flat bread).

Ingredients:
Chutney Sauce:
>2 cups mangoes
>1/2 cup cider vinegar
>1/2 cup raisins
>2 Tbsp. onion - chopped
>1 clove garlic - minced
>1/8 cup maple syrup/sweetener
>1/2 tsp. ginger (fresh grated)
>Chopped hot peppers to taste
>1/2 cup pistachios (shelled)

Tofu Filling:
>1 lb. firm tofu - mashed
>3 Tbsp. lemon juice
>1/2 tsp. salt and nutmeg
>1/4 tsp. ground, cardomon, ginger and cinnamon
>Cayenne pepper to taste

Preparation:
Chutney Sauce: In a processor, combine everything except the nuts. Pulse until it's mixed well, but not pureed. Add the nuts and pulse again. Set the mix aside.
Filling: In a mixing bowl, combine mashed tofu, lemon juice, and spices together. Mix well. *To assemble:* On a plate of greens, mound a small amount of the tofu, and ladle the mango sauce on top of it. Serve hot or cold.

Makes 4 - 6 servings

Sweet & Spicy Soybeans Over Curried Mushrooms & Rice

An Asian version of the Mexican beans and rice. A nice change of pace to the wonderfully high protein dish that everyone is used to. A great compliment to your favorite Indian dishes.

Ingredients:

> 2 cups soybeans/or any bean (soaked overnight and rinsed)
> 4 1/4 cups water
> 4 Tbsp. San-J tamari
> 1 large onion - chopped
> 1 1/2 Tbsp. arrowroot or cornstarch
> 3 Tbsp. sweet chili sauce (Asian sections or Oriental shops)
> 1 1/4 cups brown basmati rice
> 1/2 cup sliced mushrooms
> 1 tsp. curry powder

Preparation:

Boil 2 cups of water and 2 Tbsp. of tamari. Add the rice, mushrooms and curry. Cover and simmer until all the water is absorbed and the rice and mushrooms are tender. Mix together and set aside. In another pot, boil 2 cups of water. Add 2 Tbsp. of tamari, the soybeans, and onion. Cook about 30 minutes until the soybeans are tender. Reduce heat. In a separate container, mix 1/4 cup water with the arrowroot and sweet chili. Combine with the soybeans, stirring frequently until the sauce thickens. Spoon on top of the rice and serve with steamed broccoli or a salad.

Makes 4 - 6 servings

Tofu Eggplant Frittata

Traditionally known as a meat dish, we've kept the flavor, and thrown away the cholesterol and saturated fat. The tofu takes on the taste of the sauce and spices to make a delicious blend.

Ingredients:

> 2 tomatoes - seeded and chopped
> 1 lb. firm tofu - mashed
> 1 large onion - chopped
> 2 cloves garlic - minced
> 1 cup mushrooms - sliced
> 1 small zucchini - sliced thin
> 1 eggplant - peeled and cubed
> 2 Tbsp. olive oil
> 2 Tbsp. San-J tamari
> 4 Tbsp. lemon juice
> 1 tsp. sea salt
> 1/4 cup nutritional yeast/Red Star
> 1 Tbsp. paprika
> 1 tsp. each - basil, oregano and thyme

Preparation:

Heat the oil and sauté the onions, garlic, and mushrooms. Add the tamari and eggplant, and sauté 2 minutes more. Add the zucchini and tomatoes, stir in the basil, oregano, and thyme, and cook covered for 3 minutes. Uncover and cook until all the liquid is reduced. Remove from the heat and set aside. In a mixing bowl, mix the tofu, lemon juice, yeast, salt, and paprika. Mix in the eggplant sauté. In an oiled baking dish, spoon in the mixture and bake at 425° for 20 minutes. Goes great with soup and garlic bread.

Makes 4 - 6 servings

Almond Tofu

A rich nutty taste of almond comes through in this oriental style dish. I sometimes like to add a few hot peppers to give it that Szechuan Chinese flavor. Serve with rice or soba noodles.

Ingredients:

> 1 lb. firm tofu - drained, wrapped and dried
> (cut in bars 1/2 inch thick)
> 2 Tbsp. canola oil
> 1 large onion - chopped
> 1 red bell pepper
> 1/2 cup water chestnuts - drained and sliced
> 1/2 cup bamboo shoots
> 1/2 cup celery - chopped
> 1/2 cup roasted almonds (raw also acceptable)

Marinade:

> 1/2 cup water
> 3 Tbsp. San-J tamari
> 2 Tbsp. almond butter or tahini
> 1-2 cloves of garlic - minced

Glaze:

> 1/4 cup water
> 1 Tbsp. Arrowroot powder

Preparation:

Use enough oil to grill the tofu bars to a golden brown. Remove from the grill/skillet and place in a baking dish. Mix the marinade ingredients and pour over the tofu bars. Soak for at least 30 minutes, turning occasionally. Using 1/2 the marinade, sauté the onion for 2 minutes, then add the remaining ingredients, except the glaze ingredients and the tofu. Cover and cook 10 minutes on a low heat. Turn it up to a medium heat and add the tofu and the remaining marinade. Heat it for 2 minutes. Mix the water and the arrowroot together, and add to the tofu mixture. Stir constantly until the glaze thickens. Remove from the heat. Serve with either rice or noodles. Garnish with slivered almonds and chopped parsley.

Makes 4 - 6 servings

"Only in solitude do we find ourselves;
and in finding ourselves,
we find in ourselves
all our brothers in solitude."

Miguel de Unamuno

Mandarin Mock Chicken Salad

Ingredients:

    1 large can of mandarin oranges - drained (with the juice reserved)
    1/2 cup reserved juice
    3 Tbsp. agar agar - powdered
    1 1/2 cup water
    2 Tbsp. imitation chicken stock
    1/2 tsp. sea salt
    1/2 tsp. curry powder
    2 green onions - chopped
    1 lb. firm tofu - drained, cut into 1/2 inch thick pieces
    1 cup water chestnuts - sliced
    1 carrot - shredded
    Bed of spinach and arugula

Preparation:

Place the tofu in a baking dish in a single layer. In a 425° oven, bake the tofu for 20 minutes, then flip and repeat. Take 1 Tbsp. of imitation chicken stock and 3/4 cup of water and mix together. Pour over the tofu and continue to bake until almost all the liquid is absorbed. Remove and set aside. In a saucepan, combine the remaining water, agar, reserved juice, and vinegar. Bring to almost a boil, reduce heat, and simmer until all the agar is dissolved. Remove from the heat and stir in 1 Tbsp. of chicken stock, curry, and salt, and let it all cool for a minute. Stir in the remaining ingredients except the greens, and pour into a lightly oiled mold. Refrigerate until set. Loosen the mold with a rubber spatula and turn the mold out on a bed of spinach and arugula and serve.

Makes 6 - 8 servings

Marinated Tofu

This is a very basic marinade. You can add any flavors you desire. Several companies make imitation soup stocks, (i.e. chicken and beef flavors), that will allow you to imitate different meats, just by allowing the flavors to permeate and soak into the tofu.

Ingredients:

> 1 lb. firm tofu
> 1/2 cup water
> 3 Tbsp. San-J tamari
> 2 cloves garlic - minced
> 2 Tbsp. unrefined sweetener (i.e. maple syrup, date
>   sugar, fructose, etc.)
> 1 Tbsp. onion powder
> Fresh ground pepper to taste (optional)

Preparation:

Drain the tofu and wrap it in a clean dish towel. Place the cutting board on top with some weight on it and allow it to drain for 5 min. (Don't crush the tofu.) Mix all the other ingredients together and set aside. Cut the tofu into 1/2 inch thick pieces and place in a baking dish. Cover with the marinade mix and allow it to sit for at least 2 hours, turning it at least once (overnight in the refrigerator works the best, if possible). Grill the cutlets on a lightly oiled surface until they're brown on both sides or bake them at 425° for 20 minutes. Serve as a cutlet or use on a sandwich bun or bread. Eat hot or cold.

Hint: Take the remaining marinade and put it in a saucepan with a tsp. of arrowroot powder, and thicken it over a medium heat. Pour it on top of the cutlets or the sandwiches.

Makes 6 - 8 servings

Soybean, Sun Dried Tomatoes & Spinach Crostini

This low-fat treat came to me in a courtyard restaurant in Melbourne, Australia. I saw it, I reproduced it, and I liked it. How much easier can it get?

Ingredients:

- 1 cup soybeans/navy beans - soaked overnight and cooked until soft
- 1 medium onion
- 2 cloves of garlic - chopped
- 2-3 Tbsp. San-J tamari
- 1/2 cup sun dried tomatoes (soaked in water for 30 minutes - reserve the water)
- 2 Tbsp. tahini
- 8 cups spinach - rinsed and chopped
- 3 Tbsp. lemon juice
- 1/2 tsp. cayenne pepper to taste
- 6-8 whole wheat pita breads

Preparation:

In a food processor combine the soybeans, onion, garlic, tamari, tahini, and water reserved from the tomatoes. Blend well, add the cayenne and tomatoes, and pulse lightly into the mix.

In a pot, steam the spinach lightly, until tender, and cover with the lemon juice. Toast the pitas and spread the bean mixture on top of them. Cover with the spinach and serve.

Makes 6 - 8 servings

Rigatoni & Tofu with Eggplant Sauce

The secret to this dish is the tofu. Try to get it as chewy as possible. Do this by cooking the tofu on a low fire, for a long time.

Ingredients:

1 lb. firm tofu
2 large eggplants - peeled and cubed
2 large onions - chopped
4 cloves garlic - chopped
1 green bell pepper - chopped
1 red bell pepper - chopped
1 Tbsp. raw sugar/sweetener
1 Tbsp. basil
1 tsp. oregano
1 cup black olives - sliced (pitted!)
2 Tbsp. olive oil
Sea salt and fresh ground black pepper to taste
Nutritional yeast/Red Star - for garnish
1 lb. rigatoni noodles

Preparation:

In a covered skillet, heat the oil and sauté the eggplant, onions, and garlic on medium low. Cook until the eggplant becomes soft. Transfer to a blender and puree until smooth. Brown tofu cubes in the skillet, on medium low heat. Cook the tofu for 20-30 minutes, until chewy. To the tofu, add the eggplant puree and the rest of the ingredients except the pasta, olives, and yeast. Simmer the mixture for 10-15 minutes, adding water if needed. Cook the pasta as directed and drain it. To assemble, place the pasta on a platter and pour the tofu and eggplant on top. Garnish with olives and sprinkle the top with yeast.

Makes 6 servings

Spicy Tamale

This is the easiest and fastest recipe for tamales that I know. Just the kind of thing you need when the kids or your mate wants to eat Mexican food right away. While the tamales are cooking, make the rice and salad to go with it and the meal will be ready in less than one hour, everything included!

Ingredients:
Filling:
    4 cups pinto or red beans (soaked overnight, cooked and drained)
    1 large onion - chopped
    2 cloves garlic - minced
    1/2 cup black olives
    1/2 cup green olives
    1 green bell pepper - chopped
    1 cup corn kernels
    1 cup tomato sauce
    1 tsp. each - oregano, basil, cumin, chili powder
    1 tsp. olive oil

Topping:
    1 cup corn meal
    1 cup whole wheat flour
    3 Tbsp. olive oil
    3 Tbsp. maple syrup
    1 tsp. baking powder
    1 cup soy milk or nut milk
    Sea salt and fresh ground black pepper to taste

Preparation:

Filling: In a skillet, heat the oil and sauté the garlic and onions for 3 minutes. Add the remaining ingredients and sauté for another 4-5 minutes. Remove from the heat and pour in a baking dish, and set aside.

Topping: Sift all the dry ingredients together. Mix all the liquid parts well and combine with the dry batter. Pour gently on top of the filling, covering the whole top evenly. Place the mixture in a preheated oven at 350°, for 35-40 minutes.

Makes 6 - 8 servings

"Never doubt that a small group of thoughtful, committed citizens can change the world. Indeed, it's the only thing that ever has."

Margaret Mead

Ginger Soba & Broccoli with Almonds

A great noodle recipe that can be used for a main dish, or just Pa side dish. The unique blend of mirin, sesame, and sautéed ginger, makes this dish an oriental favorite. I like to serve this with marinated baked tofu and fresh (baked) spring rolls.

Ingredients:

> 1 lb. broccoli
> 1 package soba noodles (buckwheat)
> 2 Tbsp. fresh ginger - grated
> 2-3 Tbsp. San-J tamari
> 2 Tbsp. mirin/or rice syrup
> 3 green onions - chopped
> 1/4 cup almonds - blanched and slivered
> 3 cloves garlic - sliced
> 1 tsp. canola oil
> 2 Tbsp. toasted sesame seeds for garnish
> 1 tsp. sesame oil

Preparation:

Boil the soba noodles until they're tender, about 6-8 minutes. Cut the broccoli into small florets and slice up the stems Julienne style. Steam the stems for 2 minutes, then add the florets and the almonds and steam until they're tender, but still firm. (Do not overcook!) Drain the noodles and toss them with the sesame oil and mirin. Toss with the broccoli and almonds, and set the mixture aside. In a skillet, heat the oil and sauté the garlic and green onions for 2 minutes. Add the ginger and tamari and cook for 1 more minute. Add the sauté to the noodles and broccoli and toss well. Garnish it with sesame seeds and serve.

Makes 4 servings

Italian Grilled Veggies On Pasta

A touch of Northern Italy which brings to mind a quaint little bistro on a sunny Florence day. I hope this recipe turns out for you as good as the memories that it certainly brings back to me.

Ingredients:

> 6 large tomatoes - diced, with juice
> 1 Tbsp. olive oil
> 1 large onion - chopped
> 1 green bell pepper - seeded and chopped
> 1 tsp. each - garlic powder, basil, thyme, and savory
> Sea salt and fresh ground black pepper to taste
> 2 zucchini - cut in strips 1/4 inch thick
> 2 yellow crookneck squash - cut in strips 1/4 inch thick
> 1 large eggplant - peeled and cut in strips 1/4 inch thick
> Olive oil to brush the tops of the veggies with
> 1 lb. fettuccine pasta
> 1/8 cup nutritional yeast/Red Star

Preparation:

In a saucepan, combine the first 6 ingredients and bring to a boil. Reduce the heat and simmer for 20 minutes, stirring occasionally. On a baking tray, place the veggies on the tray and lightly brush them with the oil. Sprinkle them with salt and place under the broiler about 6 inches from the element. Broil until the veggies are browned, turn over, and repeat for the other side. Remove from the broiler and set aside. Boil the pasta until al dente, about 6-8 minutes, and drain. Toss the pasta and the veggies together carefully and cover with sauce. Sprinkle with the nutritional yeast and serve with a nice garlic bread.

Makes 4 - 6 servings

Quick 'N' Easy Lasagna

Here is a new twist on an age-old recipe. This will give anyone a good easy recipe to start with and to add your own variations to, creating the Italian specialty of your choice.

Ingredients:
Sauce:

> 1 lb. tomato paste and enough water to thin to desired consistency
> 1 tsp. each - garlic powder and dried basil
> 1/2 tsp. each - oregano and thyme
> Fresh ground black pepper to taste

Filling #1:

> 1 lb. firm tofu
> 1 Tbsp. San-J tamari or 1/2 tsp. sea salt
> 1 tsp. garlic powder
> 2 Tbsp. nutritional yeast/Red Star

Filling #2:

> 2 cups brown lentils (soaked, cooked and drained) or seitan ground, or fresh veggies (lightly steamed and mashed)
> 1 large onion - chopped
> 2 Tbsp. water
> 1 Tbsp. San-J tamari
> 4 cups - red and green bell peppers (hot peppers optional) - chopped

12 lasagna noodles of your choice
"Moatsarella" topping: see recipe on page 94

Preparation:
Preheat the oven to 375°. In a mixing bowl, combine all the sauce ingredients and set aside for the flavors to marry. In a large pot of boiling water, allow the noodles to cook for about 4-5 minutes till al dente (still a little firm), and remove from the heat. Rinse and leave in cold water and set aside. In another mixing bowl, mash the tofu and combine it with the rest of filling #1 ingredients. Mix together well and set aside. In a skillet, combine the tamari and water and sauté the onion and peppers for several minutes until the liquid is gone. Then add the cooked lentils and enough water to keep them from sticking to the pan. Heat several minutes, stirring frequently. Remove from the heat and set aside.

To assemble: In a deep baking dish or casserole, place a thin layer of the sauce. Place 4 lasagna noodles, side by side, to cover the whole bottom of the pan. Next, spoon the filling #2 on top and spread across the noodles until level and all the noodles are covered. Spoon some more sauce on and cover with 4 more noodles. Then, spoon on filling #1, and spread and level it also. Cover it with the last 4 noodles and pour most of the sauce that's left over the top, reserving a little sauce to spoon on top of the individual pieces as you serve them.

Prepare the Moatsarella topping as in the recipe to pour over the top of the lasagna. (Refrigerate what you don't need and use as a spread the next day on your favorite crackers or rice cakes.) Place it in the oven and bake it for 25-30 minutes or until the top is lightly browned and crisp. Serve hot with the remaining sauce.

Makes 9 large pieces or 12 normal size pieces

Chickenless Chow Mein

A quick and easy recipe using imitation chicken slices of soy or gluten, found at your local health food stores. This will make an old familiar dish. Healthy cooking doesn't have to take long.

Ingredients:

      1/2 lb. imitation chicken slices - cut in small pieces
      1 cup Chinese cabbage - coarsely chopped
      1 medium onion - sliced
      1 cup shiitake mushrooms - sliced
      1 cup bean sprouts
      1/2 cup snow peas in pods
      1/2 cup broccoli florets
      1/4 cup celery - chopped
      1 can water chestnuts - sliced
      3 Tbsp. San-J tamari
      1 Tbsp. canola oil
      2 Tbsp. arrowroot powder mixed with 1 cup of water
      1 Tbsp. imitation chicken stock/flavoring

Preparation:

In a skillet, heat the oil and sauté the onions and celery until soft. Add the imitation chicken slices, shiitake mushrooms, and chestnuts, and sauté for several more minutes. Add the broccoli, cabbage, peas, sprouts, and 1 Tbsp. of tamari, and cover. Cook for 4-5 more minutes. Add the remaining tamari and the chicken stock to the arrowroot and water, and stir well. Then pour the blend over the vegetable mix and stir continuously until the sauce thickens. Remove from the heat and serve with your favorite noodles or rice.

Makes 4 servings

Desserts
and
Treats

Classic Pie Crust

As its name indicates, you can use this crust for almost any recipe. Make a few at a time and freeze the extras. Just put wax paper in between each crust, place them in a plastic bag, and seal it.

Ingredients:

> 2 cups whole wheat flour (pastry or sifted)
> 1/3 cup canola oil
> 1/8 cup maple syrup
> 1/4 cup granulated sweetener (i.e. fructose, Sucanat, raw cane, etc.)
> 1 tsp. baking powder (non-aluminum!)
> 1/4 tsp. sea salt
> 2 Tbsp. water or juice as needed (i.e., apple, orange, pear, etc.)

Variations:

⇨Try different flours (i.e. buckwheat, graham, oat, etc.)

⇨Try different spices (i.e. cinnamon, nutmeg, allspice, ginger, etc.)

⇨Remove the sweetener and increase the salt and pepper and make a *savory* crust. Use this with quiches, pot pies and shepherd pies.

⇨For a lighter crust use 1 cup of unbleached flour to 1 cup of whole wheat flour.

Preparation:

Combine all the dry ingredients together and mix well. Add the wet ingredients and mix into a crumbly dry batter. **(Note:** In place of the maple syrup, you can use 1/4 cup of dry sweetener instead. Will make a drier batter.) Press 1/2 the batter into each pie pan. Do Not Roll! Bake in a 350° oven for 5-7 minutes, cool, and add desired filling.

Makes two 8 - 9 inch crusts

Sweet Potato Pie

Ingredients:

    3 cups sweet potatoes (peeled and steamed until soft)
    1/2 - 3/4 cup maple syrup
    1 tsp. cinnamon and nutmeg
    1/2 cup soy milk
    1 tsp. arrowroot
    Pinch of sea salt
    1/2 Classic Pie Crust (see recipe page 186)

Preparation:

Put all but the crust ingredients in a processor and blend until smooth. In a preheated 350° oven, precook the crust for 5 minutes, cool, and pour in the filling. Cook for 15-20 minutes until the crust is a rich golden brown. Remove from the oven, cool, and refrigerate. Serve with your favorite non-dairy ice cream.

Makes one pie

*"Be a friend to thyself,
and others will be so too."*

Thomas Fuller

Three Berry Pie

You can, of course, interchange any berries that you like, but whatever you do, I know it will make you BERRY happy!

Filling:

> 2 cups strawberries
> 1 1/2 cups raspberries
> 1 1/2 cups blackberries
> 2/3 cup raw sugar/fructose
> 3 Tbsp. cornstarch
> 1 tsp. lemon juice
> 1/4 cup water (more if needed)
> Pinch of salt
> Classic Pie Crust (see recipe page 186)

Preparation:

Preheat oven to 350°. In a food processor, take half the berries and all the other ingredients except for the crusts, and blend them together. In a saucepan, heat the mixture on medium heat, stirring until thick. Add the other half of the berries to the hot mix and stir in by hand. Remove and set aside. Follow the Classic Pie Crust recipe and split the batter in half. Using extra water if needed, roll out 2 crusts and fit the pie plate with one. Place the filling in the pie crust and cover it with the 2nd crust. Flute the edges with a fork and pierce holes in the top. Bake for 30 minutes or until the crust is well browned. Cool slightly and serve warm with "Nice Dream" (see recipe page 193).

Makes one pie

Tofu Cheesecake

This cheesecake recipe is 5 star! I can sit this on any dessert cart in any fancy restaurant world wide and defy anyone to tell the difference!

Ingredients:
> 1 lb. soft or silken tofu (you can omit any oil and water**)** OR 1 lb. firm tofu - add 1 tsp. oil (optional) and additional water until creamy
> 3-4 Tbsp. lemon juice
> 1/4 tsp. sea salt
> 1 Tbsp. arrowroot
> 1/2 - 3/4 cup raw sugar or fructose (can also use maple syrup if a maple taste is desired)
> 1/2 tsp. vanilla (optional)
> 1/2 Classic Pie Crust (see recipe page 186)

Preparation:
Blend all the ingredients together in a food processor until smooth, except the crust. Preheat the oven to 350°. Bake the crust for 5-7 minutes, remove from the oven, and allow to cool for 5 minutes. Fill the crust with the filling and return it to the oven for 15-20 minutes or until the tofu sets and turns a pale yellow. Remove from the oven and allow to cool, then refrigerate and serve. Top with fresh fruit or garnish before the pie cools.

Makes one pie

Coconut/Banana Cream Pie

The "Three Stooges" would never have had their famous pie throwing scene if they had this cream pie. Much too good to waste!

Ingredients:

>1/2 cup shredded coconut (extra for top sprinkle)
>3 ripe bananas
>6 Tbsp. arrowroot/cornstarch
>3 cups soy or rice milk
>3-4 Tbsp. maple syrup
>1 tsp. vanilla
>1/2 Classic Pie Crust (see recipe page 186)

Preparation:

Preheat your oven to 350°. Prepare the crust by poking it with a fork several times to release the hot air, and bake 12-15 minutes, until the crust turns a light brown. Remove from the oven and set aside to cool. In a food processor or blender, combine all the remaining ingredients except one banana and the coconut sprinkle for the top, and blend until it's smooth. Pour it into a saucepan on medium heat and heat until the mixture thickens, stirring constantly! Remove from the heat and cool for 10-15 minutes. Slice the remaining banana and cover the crust evenly with it. Pour the cooling mixture over the bananas and sprinkle with the coconut (roasted is nice). Allow the pie to cool and refrigerate.

Makes one pie

Tofu Fruit Topping

An easy blend that goes great over almost any dessert. It's a lot healthier than some of the other toppings, but certainly just as good!

Ingredients:
- 1 cup firm tofu
- 1 ripe banana - peeled
- 1 apple - peeled and cored
- 1 orange - peeled with juice
- 1/4 cup pineapple juice

Preparation:
In a blender, combine the banana, pineapple juice, apple, and orange together until smooth. Add the tofu, and again blend until smooth. Goes really great over fresh fruit, pancakes, or your favorite piece of cake. Or, add a little more liquid (water or juice) and ice, and have a great morning or afternoon drink.

Makes 3 - 4 cups

*"We can easily forgive a child
who is afraid of the dark.
The real tragedy of life
is when men are afraid of the light."*

Plato

Lemon Topping

One of the wildest times I used this sauce was over waffles. My friend had gotten me into them, and I bought a waffle maker at the flea market. I had some of this sauce in the fridge and... the rest is history!

Ingredients:

> 1/4 cup maple syrup
> 1 tsp. lemon zest (grated peel)
> 1 Tbsp. tapioca (soaked)
> 1/4 cup water
> Dash of salt
> 2 Tbsp. lemon juice

Preparation:

In a sauce pan, place the first four ingredients together and bring to a boil. Simmer for about 5 minutes, then pour into a blender along with the lemon juice and salt. Serve over fresh fruit, pancakes, or your favorite cereals.

Makes approximately 3/4 cup

*"The greatest discovery of my generation
is that human beings can alter their lives,
by altering their attitudes of mind."*

William James

Nice Dream

This frozen treat has ice cream beat in every way! (Except the fat, sodium, sugar, and cholesterol levels!) What a way to get your potassium, and so delicious too!

Ingredients:

> 4-5 very ripe frozen bananas
> (freeze them without skins!)
> Your choice of extracts or essential oils, frozen fruit,
> non-dairy chocolate chips, nuts, or any other
> thing you can think of!

Preparation:

Cut the frozen bananas in small chunks and place in your food processor. As you blend the bananas, you'll have to keep moving them off the sides with a rubber spatula, when the machine is stopped, until it's creamy. Then add whatever other ingredients you wish, and process until they're all mixed together. Eat it immediately.

Note: Nice Dream will melt and cannot be refrozen without losing the creamy consistency.

Makes 4 - 6 servings

*"It is man's sympathy with all creatures
that first makes him truly a man."*

Albert Schweitzer

Chocolate or Carob Toppings

This is a great replacement for the old style syrups. I've taken out the oils and the dairy, but left the sweet goodness behind. Isn't that what we really wanted all along, anyway?

Ingredients:

> 1 cup water
> 2-3 Tbsp. sweetener
>   (raw sugar, maple syrup, dates, rice syrup, etc.)
> 1 rounded Tbsp. cocoa powder or carob powder
> 1 Tbsp. arrowroot
> 1/4 tsp. sea salt
> 1-2 tsp. vanilla

Preparation:

Combine all the ingredients in a blender, and blend until smooth. Pour into a sauce pan and heat, on a medium heat, until the sauce begins to thicken. Remove it from the heat, cool, and chill, or use it hot over pastries, pancakes, or your favorite non-dairy frozen desserts, like Nice Dream (see recipe page 193)!

Makes 1 cup

"Wise men talk because they have something to say;
fools, because they have to say something."

Plato

Cashew Cream

A great topping for any of your favorite desserts. Put a big dollop in your next mug of hot cocoa. Yummm!

Ingredients:
> 1/2 cup raw cashews
> 1/2 cup water
> 2 Tbsp. canola oil
> 1 tsp. vanilla
> 1-2 Tbsp. fructose/raw sugar (sweeten to your taste)
> Pinch of sea salt

Preparation:
Soak the nuts in the water for 30 minutes or more. Place them both in a strong blender or processor and blend until creamy, adding water if needed. (Several minutes.) Add the remaining ingredients and blend for several more minutes. Refrigerate and serve when cooled. If needed, you can refresh and fluff it up by placing it back in the blender for a few seconds. Place a dollop on your favorite pie, pudding, etc.

Makes approximately 1 cup

"First it was necessary to civilize man
in relation to man.
Now it is necessary to civilize man
in relation to nature and animals."

Victor Hugo

Tofu Cream

This was invented to take the place of whipped cream for my daughter and my friends. I felt I had to create something for them. So enjoy!

Ingredients:

1/2 lb. firm tofu – rinsed and undrained
3-4 Tbsp. maple syrup
1 tsp. vanilla
1 Tbsp. canola oil
Pinch of sea salt

Preparation:

Place all the ingredients in a food processor or blender and whip it until it's smooth and creamy. You may have to use a rubber spatula to push it down the sides as you blend. (Make sure the machine is off!) Use as a topping, icing, or just a dollop on your favorite treats.

Makes about 1 cup

"How narrow we selfish, conceited creatures
are in our sympathies!
How blind to the rights of all the rest of creation!"

John Muir

Pineapple Tofu Baklava

This recipe may take a little time, but the results are well worth it. One of the sweetest desserts I know. Serve this with your favorite Middle Eastern or Mediterranean dinners.

Ingredients:
>2 cups firm tofu - mashed
>20 oz. can - crushed pineapple in syrup
>3/4 cup Sucanat/raw sugar
>1 Tbsp. lemon zest
>1 Tbsp. lemon juice
>1/2 lb. filo pastry leaves (8 leaves)
>1/2 tsp. sea salt
>1/4 - 1/2 cup canola oil - (for brushing leaves)
>1/4 - 1/2 cup maple syrup

Preparation:
In a food processor, combine the tofu, lemon zest, juice, salt, and sugar together. Mix well. Drain the pineapple, reserving the syrup, and add enough of the syrup to make the tofu mix creamy, but not runny. By hand, stir in the pineapple and set aside. Take one leaf of the filo, keeping the other leaves moist under a damp towel, and place in a 9" x 13' baking pan. Brush with canola oil and repeat with 3 more leaves, stacking them on top of each other. Spoon on the tofu mix and spread evenly. Repeat the same method as before with the filo leaves, sandwiching the tofu. In a preheated 350° oven, bake for 20 minutes, brush with maple syrup, and cook for 15 more minutes or until browned. Remove from the oven, brush again with maple syrup, and cut in triangles or diamond shapes. Cool and serve.

Makes 12 pieces
(but feeds 6 people, 'cause everyone wants seconds!)

Walnut Ginger Bread

This recipe was adapted from a friend's recipe, that used dairy and eggs. She was so surprised when her redesigned recipe came out well, that she immediately cut egg and dairy out of most of her other recipes, too. Easy, huh?

Ingredients:

> 1 1/2 cups whole wheat flour
> 3 Tbsp. canola oil
> 1/2 cup orange juice
> 1 rounded tsp. ginger (ground)
> 1/2 cup maple syrup/palm sugar
> 1 tsp. nutmeg
> 1/2 tsp. baking soda
> 1/2 cup walnuts - crushed
> Pinch of sea salt

Preparation:

In a mixing bowl, sift together all the dry ingredients except the walnuts. In a separate bowl, combine all the wet ingredients. Combine wet and dry batters together and mix in the nuts. Pour into an oiled and floured loaf pan and place in a preheated oven at 350° for 25-30 minutes. Check the middle with a toothpick. It should come out clean when done. Cool on a rack and top with Tofu Cream (page 196), if desired.

Makes 6 - 8 servings

Sesame Maple Cookies

A nice sesame taste without being overly sweet. A little like eating an Italian biscotti. Good for tea and snack time.

Ingredients:

> 1 cup whole wheat flour
> 1 cup organic unbleached flour
> 1 cup sesame seeds
> 1/2 cup maple syrup (3/4 if sweetener desired)
> 1/4 cup canola oil
> 1/8 cup tahini
> Pinch of salt
> 1 tsp. baking powder

Preparation:

In a large bowl, combine the flour, seeds, salt, and baking powder together. In a separate bowl, whisk the oil, maple syrup, and tahini together. Mix the wet and dry parts together to make a stiff batter. Roll the batter into about 20-25 small balls. On a non-oiled cookie sheet, place the small balls of batter and flatten down a little. Place in a preheated oven at 350° for about 12-15 minutes, or until nicely browned. Remove from the oven and place on a rack until they're cool enough to eat!

Makes 20 - 25 cookies

"The obvious is that which is never seen,
until someone expresses it simply."

Khalil Gibran

Chocolate Chip Cookies

These are quick and easy, two words that go very well together when we're dealing with cookies. Let the kids help make them, and make sure they help clean up before tasting the results!

Ingredients:

>   2 cups whole wheat flour
>   3/4 cup raw sugar
>   1/3 cup canola oil
>   1 tsp. baking powder
>   2 tsp. vanilla
>   1 cup non-dairy chocolate chips
>   1/2 cup walnuts - chopped (optional)
>   2 Tbsp. applesauce
>   Pinch of sea salt
>   2 Tbsp. orange juice/apple juice

Preparation:

Sift the dry ingredients into a large bowl. In a small bowl, combine the oil, vanilla, and applesauce, and whisk together. Combine with the dry part and mix well into a stiff batter. Add the walnuts and chips and mix in thoroughly. Place a large Tbsp. of the batter on an un-oiled cookie tray. Repeat, leaving about 2" between each cookie. Place in a preheated 350° oven for about 12 minutes, or until golden brown. Remove from the oven and place on a rack until they're cool enough to eat!

Makes 20 - 25 cookies

Rice Chewies

A favorite in any household with kids (or a sweet tooth). These are not only easy, but fun to make too. Let the children help you. If you place the chewies in a sealed container, they'll stay crisp for a while.

Ingredients:

1 cup brown basmati rice - cooked
3 Tbsp. maple syrup
1/3 cup cashews - chopped
1/3 cup raisins or chopped dates
1/4 cup soy flour
2 Tbsp. arrowroot
1/2 tsp. nutmeg
1 tsp. vanilla
1/4 tsp. sea salt
Water if needed

Preparation:

Mix all the ingredients together in a big bowl, trying not to break the rice too much. On a lightly oiled cookie tray, place small amounts of the batter rolled into little balls. Flatten down to about a 1/2" in thickness, leaving space between each chewy. Bake 45 minutes at 200°, or until lightly browned. Cool and refrigerate. Great for breakfast, snacks, or parties.

Makes 15 - 20 chewies

Spiced Almond Apples

A favorite for the autumn harvest (or anytime). Make this low fat treat for the kids, or your best get together. Certain to be appreciated by all.

Ingredients:

> 6 apples - peeled, cored and cubed
> 1/2 cup almonds - sliced or slivered
> 1/4 tsp. ground clove
> 1 tsp. nutmeg
> 3/4 cup maple syrup/rice or malt syrup
> 1/2 cup soft tofu
> 1/2 tsp. almond extract

Preparation:

On a baking tray, spread and roast the almonds for 8-10 minutes at 350°, or until they're browned. Remove and set aside.

In a baking dish, spread the apples and sprinkle them with clove and 1/2 cup of the maple syrup (save the other 1/4 cup for later). Cover and bake for about 15 minutes at 350°, or until the apples are tender. Remove the apples and stir, making sure everything is coated well. In a blender, combine the tofu and almond extract and blend until it's smooth and creamy. To serve, place the equivalent of 1 apple into a bowl. Sprinkle with some almonds, then top with a dollop of the tofu cream. Sprinkle with some nutmeg, drizzle on a little maple syrup, and serve!

Makes 6 servings

Hawaiian Fruit Salad
with Tofu Cream

The tropics come to life with the sweet taste of all these Hawaiian favorites. With or without the cream, it's a healthy, delicious treat.

Ingredients:

2 large papayas - seeded, and scooped out
3 bananas- peeled and sliced
2 large avocados - cut in small cubes
2 cups lychees - peeled and seeded, or seedless
  grapes - washed
1/2 cup sunflower seeds - hulled
1 kiwi fruit for garnish - peeled and sliced

Topping:

1 cup soft tofu
2 Tbsp. lemon juice
3 - 4 Tbsp. maple syrup
Pinch of sea salt
1/2 tsp. vanilla

Preparation:

Combine all the fruit in a bowl and sprinkle with the sunflower seeds. In a blender, combine all the topping ingredients and blend until creamy smooth. Pour the topping over the fruit and garnish it with kiwi slices.

Makes 4 - 6 servings

Sweet Rice & Figs
with Baked Tofu Icing

Ingredients:

>   1 cup white basmati rice
>   1 3/4 cups water
>   1 1/2 cups dry figs (Mission) - stemmed and soaked
>   (retain the soak water)
>   1/2 tsp. of the following: nutmeg, cinnamon, cloves
>   1/2 cup maple syrup or rice syrup
>   1 cup soaked water from the figs
>   1 cup silken firm tofu
>   2 Tbsp. fructose/raw sugar
>   1/2 tsp. pure vanilla extract
>   Mint leaves for garnish

Preparation:

In a pot, boil the water and add the rice. Reduce the heat, cover, and simmer until all the water is absorbed, about 20 minutes. Fluff with a fork and set aside. Drain and reserve the liquid from the figs. Place the rice in a baking dish and press it flat and even like a thick crust. Cut the figs in half and place them on top of the rice. In a mixing bowl, add 1 cup of the soak water, the maple syrup, nutmeg, cinnamon, and cloves. Mix well and pour over the figs and rice. In a preheated 350° oven, place the mixture, uncovered, into the oven and bake for 15 minutes. In a blender or processor, mix the tofu, fructose, and vanilla until smooth. Pour over the figs and rice mixture, and bake for 15 more minutes, or until the tofu starts to brown. Remove and cool. Cut it into squares, garnish with mint, or refrigerate and eat chilled.

Makes 8 - 12 servings

Cashew Crunches

This treat can be made quickly anytime in a half hour or less.
They also keep very well . . . I think. They've never been around
long enough for me to really find out.

Ingredients:

> 1 cup cashews
> 1 cup whole wheat flour
> 1 cup rolled oats
> 1 cup rice flour
> 1 cup maple syrup
> 1/3 cup canola oil
> 1/4 cup soymilk (more if needed)
> Pinch of salt
> 1 tsp. baking powder (non-aluminum)

Preparation:

In a processor, combine all the dry ingredients except the
cashews. Combine the cashews and the other ingredients
and blend, on pulse, until all the ingredients have mixed
into a thick batter. Shape the batter into little balls and
place on a cookie sheet. Preheat the oven to 350°. Place
the rolled batter into the oven for 20 minutes or until brown
on the outside. Remove from the oven and allow to cool.

Makes 25 - 30 balls

"In a gentle way, you can shake the world."

Mahatma Gandhi

Tofu Banana Date Pudding

This is a great, easy dessert that everyone loves. If you really want to be decadent, you can eat it with fresh baked vanilla cookies instead of spoons!

Ingredients:
 1 lb. firm tofu
 2 ripe bananas
 1/2 cup dates - pitted and chopped
 2 Tbsp. maple syrup
 1 tsp. vanilla
 1/8 cup tahini or nut butter
 2 Tbsp. water
 1 Tbsp. canola oil (optional - omit to lower fat)

Preparation:
In a food processor, combine and blend all the ingredients together until smooth. Spoon into individual serving size containers and chill.

Makes 4 - 6 servings

"We do not inherit the earth from our ancestors, we merely borrow it from our children."

Chief Tecumsuh

Apricot (or any other jam) Bars

These are great for snacks or for packed lunches. It's good to make a double batch of these 'cause they go so fast.

Ingredients:

2 cups sifted cake meal or whole wheat flour
1/4 cup canola oil
Natural fruit juice - just enough to hold dough together
1 cup raw sugar or fructose
1 tsp. vanilla
1 10-12 oz. jar apricot preserves
1/4 cup lemon juice
1/2 cup walnuts or pecans - chopped

Preparation:
In a mixing bowl, combine the cake meal and the sweetener together. Whisk the oil, vanilla, and the fruit juice together. Combine the wet and dry batters together and form into a dough. Press 3/4 of the dough onto the bottom of a greased baking pan. Pat it down flat. Preheat the oven to 350°. Place in the oven and bake for 10 minutes. Place the remaining dough in the freezer for the 10 minutes. In a mixing bowl, combine the preserves and lemon juice. Spread the apricot mix on the hot crust. Sprinkle with the nuts and crumble the rest of the pastry dough over the top. Bake for 30-35 minutes, or until brown. Remove from the oven and cut into squares when cool.

Makes approximately 12 pieces

Tofu Coconut Cake

Adapted from a Filipino recipe. I've taken out the milk and eggs, and without the animal fat, the coconut isn't nearly as fattening. So enjoy, Bro (or Sister)!

Ingredients:

- 1/2 cup soft or silken tofu
- 1 1/2 cups whole wheat pastry flour
- 1 tsp. baking powder (aluminum free)
- 1/2 cup coconut - shredded
- 1 cup soy, rice, or nut milk
- 1/4 cup canola oil
- 1/4 cup soy flour
- 3/4 - 1 cup coconut or palm sugar (found at Asian shops or health food stores)

Preparation:

In a food processor or large mixing bowl, combine the tofu, soy milk, oil, sweeteners, and coconut together until smooth and creamy. Combine the remaining ingredients together and mix into the coconut mixture, forming a nice wet batter. Pour into an oiled and floured cake pan and bake in a preheated 350° oven for 45 minutes, or until a toothpick pulls out clean from the center. Remove from the oven and allow to cool. Can be eaten as is or covered with your choice of frosting.

Makes 12 - 15 pieces

Crème-Filled Crumb Cake

Ingredients:

First layer: *Mix together:*
>   1/2 cup raw sugar or fructose
>   1/2 tsp. salt
>   1 cup whole wheat pastry flour
>   1/2 cup walnuts - chopped
>   Press this mixture into the bottom of a deep baking pan.

Second layer: *Mix together in a food processor:*
>   1 lb. tofu (firm)
>   3 Tbsp. oil
>   1/2 cup sugar
>   2 Tbsp. whole wheat pastry flour
>   1/2 tsp. salt
>   Spread on top of first layer.

Third layer: *Process till smooth:*
>   1/2 lb. tofu (soft)
>   3 Tbsp. lemon juice
>   1/4 cup oil
>   1/2 tsp. salt
>   1 cup raw sugar
>   1 cup water

Flour Mixture: *Mix together in a bowl:*
>   2 cups whole wheat pastry flour
>   1/2 tsp. each - baking soda and cinnamon
>   2 tsp. baking powder
>   1/2 cup chopped walnuts

Preparation:

Preheat the oven to 350°. Stir blended ingredients for
the third layer into flour mixture until there are no lumps.
Spread this over the second layer, being careful not to stir
the second and third layers together. Bake 40-45 minutes,
then let sit for 5 minutes. Loosen edges and turn onto a
plate or platter. Cool before slicing.

Makes 12 servings

Basic Chocolate Cake

Made this for a party not long ago, but I added a 1/2 dozen passion fruits to the icing recipe. Wow! What a great idea!

Ingredients:

      3 cups whole wheat pastry flour
      1/2 cup canola oil
      2 cups sweetener of your choice (note that the flavors can vary by the sweetener)
      1 cup soft tofu
      3/4 cup cocoa powder
      1/2 tsp. sea salt
      1/2 Tbsp. baking powder (non - aluminum)
      1 1/2 cups rice or soy milk
      1 tsp. vanilla

Icing:

      1/4 cup tahini
      1/4 cup firm tofu
      1/2 cup maple syrup/other liquid sweetener
      1-2 Tbsp. cocoa powder
      Water if needed to thin

Preparation:

In a large bowl, sift all the dry ingredients together and set aside. In a blender, combine all the remaining ingredients, adding the oil in last. Blend until smooth and combine it with the dry ingredients. Mix together well and fold equally into 2 round, oiled, and floured cake pans. Bake in a preheated 350° oven for about 35-40 minutes, or until a toothpick pulls out clean from the center. (Cakes may crack a little on top; just fill and cover with the icing.)

Remove from the oven and take out of the cake pans.
Set on a rack and allow them to cool. In a food processor,
blend all the icing ingredients until smooth. Refrigerate it
for at least 1 hour. Take one round cake, spread a layer of
icing on top, and place the other cake on top of it. Cover
the whole thing with the remaining icing and serve.

Makes 8 or more servings

*"I think that everything connected
with vegetarianism is of the highest importance,
because there will never be any peace in this world
so long as we eat animals.
I think animals are just as much God's creatures
as men are, and we have to respect them,
and love them,
not slaughter them."*

Issac Bashevis Singer

Walnut Oat Cake
with Chocolate Frosting

I've taken all the oil out of this one. Now you can have a guilt-free cake. Won't the kids be surprised to hear you say they can have seconds?

Ingredients:
> 1 cup rolled oats
> 1 cup walnuts - chopped
> 1 1/2 cups soy, rice or nut milk
> 1/2 cup apple sauce
> 1 1/2 cups whole wheat pastry flour
> 1 tsp. baking powder
> 1 1/2 cups maple syrup
> 2 Tbsp. tahini
> 1/2 tsp. each - cinnamon, nutmeg, and sea salt
> 1/2 cup semi-sweet dark chocolate chips (non-dairy!)

Preparation:
Heat milk to almost boiling and remove instantly. Pour in the oats and allow them to soak until lukewarm. In a food processor, combine the oats with all the remaining ingredients except the chocolate chips, and blend them till smooth. Pour the batter into a floured cake pan. Bake in a preheated 350° oven for 45 minutes, or until a toothpick pulls out clean from the center. Before removing from the oven, place the chocolate chips on top for 30-40 seconds. Remove from the oven and immediately spread the chocolate evenly on top. Allow it to cool on a rack before slicing.

Makes 8 wedges

Convenient Coffee Cake

It's just as the name implies. You can whip this up so fast and easy; but don't tell your guests. Let them think you slaved away just for them, and it can be your secret.

Ingredients:
>2 cups whole wheat pastry flour
>1 cup raw sugar or fructose
>1 cup raisins
>1 1/4 cups water
>1/3 cup canola oil (You can replace 1/4 cup of the oil with 1/4 cup of apple sauce for less fat.)
>1 tsp. each - baking powder, baking soda, and cinnamon
>1/2 tsp. each - ground cloves, nutmeg, and sea salt
>1/2 cup walnuts

Preparation:
In a bowl, sift all the dry ingredients together. In a blender or bowl, whisk all the other ingredients together and combine them with the dry part. Fold the mixture into an oiled and floured baking pan or coffee ring, and bake in a preheated oven at 350° for 45 minutes, or until a toothpick pulls out clean from the center. Cool and serve with your favorite herbal tea or coffee substitute.

Makes 8 or more servings

Old Fashioned Fruitcake

Now, this is the kind you can really eat. I remember those plastic wrapped fruitcakes you used to get as tips from people on the holidays. They made good bookends and doorstops. This, on the other hand, is moist and delicious. Enjoy!

Ingredients:

> 3 1/2 cups whole wheat flour
> 2 cups maple syrup/sweetener
> 1/2 cup canola oil
> 1 cup firm tofu
> 1 1/2 cups water
> 1/4 cup tahini
> 1/2 cup each - raisins, walnuts, chopped dates, and
>   cherries (pitted and halved)
> 1 Tbsp. each - lemon and orange zest (grated peel)
> 1 tsp. almond extract
> 1/2 tsp. each - baking soda, baking powder,
>   nutmeg, and sea salt

Preparation:

In a bowl, sift together the flour, baking soda and powder, and salt. In a blender, combine the tofu and the water together. Add everything else, except the raisins, nuts, dates, and cherries, to the blender, and blend at a slow speed until it's creamy smooth. Combine the blender mix with the dry part and mix thoroughly. Mix in the remaining ingredients and stir well. Pour the batter into 2 rectangular bread pans, or one large oiled and floured, cake pan. Bake in a preheated oven at 350° for 30-35 minutes, or until a toothpick pulls out clean from the center. Cool it on a rack. (Can be served with an icing of choice, if desired.)

Makes 12 - 15 slices

Maple Walnut Carrot Cake

I've tried a lot of carrot cakes, and most of them are too dry for me. To remedy this, I've added both tofu and applesauce. This keeps my version nice and moist.

Ingredients:

2 1/2 cups whole wheat flour
3 cups carrots - grated
1 cup walnuts - chopped
1/3 cup canola oil
1/2 cup applesauce
2 cups maple syrup/sweetener
2 tsp. vanilla
1 tsp. each - baking powder, baking soda, and cinnamon
1 cup soft tofu
1/4 cup orange juice
1/4 tsp. sea salt

Preparation:

Combine all the dry ingredients together and set aside. In a food processor, combine the tofu, oil, applesauce, maple syrup, and orange juice together, and blend until smooth. In a big mixing bowl, pour in the tofu blend and stir in the dry part. Mix in the carrots and the nuts. Pour into an oiled and floured cake pan, and place in a preheated oven at 350° for about 45 minutes, or until a toothpick pulls out clean from the center. Cool slightly and turn out on to a rack to cool. Add icing if desired and serve.

Makes 16 - 20 servings

Easy Carrot Cake

One of people's favorite desserts. If you get good sweet organic carrots, sprinkle a little grated carrot on top for a nice garnish.

Ingredients:

2 cups whole wheat flour
2 cups unbleached flour
2/3 cup canola oil
1 cup maple syrup/sweetener
3 cups organic carrots - grated
1 cup walnuts - chopped
1/2 cup dates - chopped
1 Tbsp. baking powder
1 tsp. baking soda
1 tsp. cinnamon
1/2 tsp. nutmeg
1 1/2 cups rice milk or soy milk
Tofu icing optional: (combine tofu, sweetener to taste, vanilla, and a pinch of salt. Keep it thick!)

Preparation:

Sift all the dry ingredients together, mix all the wet ingredients together, and then combine the two. Add the nuts, carrots, and dates, mix well, and fold into an oiled and floured cake pan. Bake in a preheated oven at 350° for 30-40 minutes, or until a toothpick comes out clean when sticking it in the center. If using the tofu icing, spread it on the top about 10 minutes before the cake is finished and allow it to bake on.

Makes 12 - 15 servings

Tofu Hot Fudge/Candy

For the sweet tooth junkies that crave chocolate, here it is! Only now with a lot less fat, and no cholesterol. Gee, I hope I didn't take all the fun out of it for you. Pour this over "Nice Dream" - it's simply fabulous!

Ingredients:

 1/4 cup - unsweetened dark chocolate
 1/2 cup tahini
 1/3 cup unsweetened cocoa powder
 1 1/2 cup fructose/raw sugar/palm sugar
 1 cup silken firm tofu
 1 tsp. vanilla

Preparation:

In a double boiler, melt the chocolate. Add the cocoa and tahini, and mix until smooth. Add the fructose and simmer for 25 minutes. In a processor or blender, put in the tofu and blend until creamy. Add the tofu to the chocolate blend and stir constantly for 3-4 minutes. Add the vanilla and stir until it's well blended. Can be used at this point for a hot topping, or pour it into an oiled baking dish to about a 1" thickness and allow it to cool and firm up. Cut it into small squares and place it in the freezer. Allow it to get hard. You can also keep it in the fridge, but it won't be quite as hard.

Makes approximately 25 pieces

Chocolate Raspberry Creme Pie

While staying at my friend's beach house, I was inspired to create this as a change from the "cheesecakes" I was always making. Great for all you chocolate lovers, so enjoy!

Ingredients:

Crust:

> 3/4 cup whole wheat flour
> 3/4 cup unbleached self raising flour
> 1/3 cup canola oil
> 1/2 cup unrefined sweetener (i.e. coconut, palm, date, or raw sugars)
> 2 Tbsp. orange juice
> Pinch of sea salt

Filling:

> 12 oz. firm tofu
> 10 oz. any "all natural" raspberry preserve or jam
> 3-4 Tbsp. cocoa powder
> 1/2 cup unrefined sweetener (more if a sweeter pie is desired)
> 1/4 tsp. citric acid
> Enough water to make the filling creamy
> 1 tsp. arrowroot powder

Preparation:

Crust: In a mixing bowl, sift the dry ingredients together. Combine the oil and orange juice and add it to the dry ingredients. Mix it until you get a dry crumbly batter. Press it by hand into a large pie plate or shallow cake pan. In a preheated 350° oven, bake the crust for about 5-7 minutes, or until the edges start to brown. Remove it from the oven and allow it to cool for a few minutes.

Filling: Combine all the ingredients in a food processor and blend until they're smooth and creamy. Pour the filling into the cooled pie crust and return it to the oven as before. Place it for 5 minutes on the bottom rack, then transfer it to the top rack and bake it for another 10 minutes, or until the filling has set. Remove it and allow it to cool, then refrigerate it until you're ready to serve. You can garnish it with tofu or cashew cream and mint leaves.

Makes 1 large pie

"Thou shalt not kill,
does not apply to murder of one's own kind only,
but to all living beings.
This commandment was inscribed
in the human breast long before
it was proclaimed on Sinai."

Count Leo Tolstoy

Index

V

W